Endorsements of *The Secrets o*

Drawing from a lifetime of extraordinary experiences in business, civic engagement, and the Presbyterian Church, Dr. Frank Clark Spencer presents a thoughtful and persuasive case for navigating modern life with purpose and integrity. Intelligent, forthright, and concise, *The Secrets of Success* distills three timeless principles—commitment, compassion, curiosity—that can help anyone thrive.

Whether you're looking for a new direction, a fresh challenge, or a renewed sense of purpose, *The Secrets of Success* offers motivating guidance to help you pursue a life of balance, fulfillment, and lasting happiness.

RICHARD DUBOSE, President of Montreat Conference Center

Frank has been my friend and colleague for over 40 years, and I can say with confidence that he has outlined a compelling blueprint for a life where prosperity serves a greater purpose: doing good in the world. His journey—rooted in love and service to family, faith and community—is shared with clarity and insight.

While generations may change, his wisdom remains timeless. I highly recommend this book to both the 17-year-old just starting out and the 60-plus-year-old reflecting on their path. No matter your age, you'll find valuable lessons in Frank's reflections.

MIKE CLEMENT, Founder and Managing Partner, Strait Insights; former Chief of Global Communications, Bank of America

Reflecting on the arc of his remarkable career as a leader and pastor, Frank's personal retrospective is a gift to anyone seeking a life of purpose and meaning—without losing themselves or the relationships that matter most.

Between buildings and boardrooms, deals and negotiations, marriage and children, he uncovers essential truths found in the depths and breadth of one man's quest for success and happiness.

REV. DR. LORI RAIBLE, Pastor, Selwyn Presbyterian Church; Trustee, Union Presbyterian Seminary

The Secrets of Success is neither a self-help nor "get rich quick" book. Part personal reflection of well-lived life and part holistic book of wisdom, Spencer offers a compass and maps through a beautifully told series of life journeys that show how the trip can—and should—be as meaningful as the destination. Drawing on his impressive accomplishments and honest reflections on setbacks, Spencer shares time-tested principles for anyone seeking meaningful success in life and work.

He honors the uniqueness of each generation, encouraging readers to deeply consider their preparation, pursuit, and goals—not just to find what they think they want, but to discover what's truly worth living for: fulfillment, purpose, service, and significance.

Spencer reminds us that fun, adventure, finding the right life-partner, and nurturing spiritual convictions in community are just as important as education and professional skills. Perhaps most refreshing, many of the book's most encouraging values come toward the end—graciously showing us that at any age or stage, we can take thoughtful steps to improve our path. Spencer reveals that the best and most rewarding kinds of success truly can be yours.

REV. THOMAS TAYLOR, J.D., Ph.D., President & CEO, Presbyterian Foundation

I often tell people to "make the rest of your life the best of your life." Going forward, I'm simply going to tell them to read *The Secrets of Success*. What a compelling, riveting journey. In this concise and powerful read, Dr. Spencer takes you through his extraordinary life, offering practical tips, insights, and tools for building a successful, meaningful, and rewarding life.

Looking for lessons on drive, ambition, independence, or confidence? They're here. Want a fresh perspective on leadership, finances, education, construction, real estate, relationships, religion, athletics, parenting, travel, or diversity, equity and inclusion? Grab a pen and pad— this book delivers.

As an educator, speaker and coach, I'm always seeking resources to strengthen my message. Going forward, every client and coachee of mine will be encouraged to read this book. While reading, I found myself thinking, "Why didn't Dr. Spencer write this sooner? My life could have been very different." His take on excellence, service, discomfort, preparation, and long-term success is spot on.

That said, this book isn't for everyone. It's for those ready to look in the mirror and challenge themselves— personally and professionally—to go beyond the next level. I'm going to be better, do better and live better because of *The Secrets of Success*.

DR. JAMES SMITH, Jr., CSP, Author, Speaker, Educator, Coach

THE SECRETS OF SUCCESS

THE **SECRETS** OF **SUCCESS**

How to build a great career and live a happy life

Reverend Dr. Frank Clark Spencer

GRAMMAR
FACTORY
— EST⁰ 2013 —

Published by Grammar Factory Publishing,
an imprint of MacMillan Company Limited.

Grammar Factory Publishing
MacMillan Company Limited
25 Telegram Mews, 39th Floor, Suite 3906
Toronto, Ontario, Canada
M5V 3Z1

www.grammarfactory.com

Spencer, Rev. Dr. Frank Clark.
The Secrets of Success: How to build a great career
and live a happy life / Rev. Dr. Frank Clark Spencer.

Paperback ISBN 978-1-998528-27-1
eBook ISBN 978-1-998528-28-8

1. BUS071000 - BUSINESS & ECONOMICS / Leadership.
2. BUS097000 - BUSINESS & ECONOMICS / Workplace Culture.
3. BUS012000 - BUSINESS & ECONOMICS / Careers / General.

Production Credits
Cover design by Designerbility
Interior layout design by Setareh Ashrafologhalai
Book production and editorial services
by Grammar Factory Publishing

Grammar Factory's Carbon Neutral Publishing Commitment
Grammar Factory Publishing is proud to be neutralizing the
carbon footprint of all printed copies of its authors' books printed by
or ordered directly through Grammar Factory or its affiliated companies
through the purchase of Gold Standard-Certified International Offsets.

Disclaimer
The material in this publication is of the nature of general comment
only and does not represent professional advice. It is not intended
to provide specific guidance for particular circumstances, and it should
not be relied on as the basis for any decision to take action or not take
action on any matter which it covers. Readers should obtain professional
advice where appropriate, before making any such decision. To the
maximum extent permitted by law, the author and publisher disclaim
all responsibility and liability to any person, arising directly
or indirectly from any person taking or not taking
action based on the information in this publication.

For my wife, Melanie, who has been my partner, my closest advisor, my greatest supporter, my love, and my friend for forty-four years.

And for my children, Aly and Clark, who have shown me new ways to see the world and who have taught me how to be a better person, a better father, an advisor, and their greatest supporter.

CONTENTS

INTRODUCTION
PRINCIPLES THAT
LEAD TO SUCCESS

There are universal truths that lie at the heart of creating a successful career and a happy life. These include commitment to a life partner, an employer, and cultural institutions. I can certainly see their efficacy in my own history. Some of these principles may seem counterintuitive to our current cultural moment, because they do not embrace a focus on individual self-actualization or the gig economy, but all are backed up by research. For example, you don't build career success by constantly switching jobs, but rather by realizing significant accomplishments. I have stayed in some jobs as little as two years, and never stayed in the same job more than fifteen years, but in all of my roles I stayed until I achieved the goals I had established with my organization.

I have been fortunate to live an extraordinary life based on the principles that I will share with you in these pages. Sometimes I was in the right place at the right time. Other times, perhaps I was lucky. But more often than not, I was willing to put myself forward, to get noticed, to take a risk. By definition, not all risks work out, but taking no risks will not achieve any positive outcomes. Anyone can put these principles to work in their own life and build a successful career and a happy life.

Throughout my life, beginning in early adolescence and carrying through to today in my mid-sixties, four elements have always been present for me: family, faith, community, and vocation/finance.

Yes, finance. This is not a book about wealth creation or how to get rich quick, but it will discuss subjects related to career and financial matters, because in the United States of today some level of financial security and professional mastery is required for other elements of life to be in balance.

According to the US Department of Labor, the average employed person in the US works 8.08 hours each workday. That equals 40.4 hours per week, 2,020 hours per year, 80,000 hours over a career, or about 36% of our waking time as adults. For many who achieve at high levels, the percentage only gets higher. Given that Americans spend so much of their time and emotional energy on their careers, insights leading to positive outcomes are essential for success and happiness. However, the principles we will examine extend far beyond career implications.

The Harvard Study of Adult Development concludes:

"There is a lot to be said for achievement if what you're doing is meaningful to you. What we find is that the badges of achievement don't make people happy. We had people who were CEOs,

who made lots of money, or who became famous. Those things did not relate to happiness. But, to the extent that achieving things that are important to you is fulfilling, that does make a difference in well-being."

First and foremost, my wife, Melanie, and I have built a life partnership that has lasted over forty years and is the platform that has allowed each of us to achieve things that neither of us could have done, or even attempted, alone. We have had financial success as a result of our partnership, moving from a negative net worth coming out of graduate school to a place of financial security today. Sometimes I was the primary breadwinner, while Melanie fulfilled that role in our family at many other times.

We have been lifelong learners, each earning multiple graduate degrees, including doctorates as a part of second careers. That continuous learning has allowed Melanie to transition from a senior marketing role in the nation's largest bank to becoming a research scientist and building the Center for Outcomes Research and Evaluation in the nation's second-largest public health system.

For my part, I have led four not-for-profit organizations as the president or CEO, as well as four profit-seeking businesses, including an initial public offering (IPO) on the New York Stock Exchange (NYSE). Those organizations have employed thousands of people.

Extraordinary success in business saw the small private company I bought into grow from forty employees with a valuation of $10 million, to over 600 employees and a publicly traded valuation in excess of $1 billion. I was named Southeast Entrepreneur of the Year in the real estate and construction category, and later was inducted into the Ernst & Young (E&Y) national Entrepreneur Hall of Fame.

After leaving the company that I took public, I entered seminary, earned a master's degree, and changed careers to full-time ministry. Throughout our lives, we have been committed to professional success, to our community, to the Presbyterian Church, to our families and to each other. While no life is without its ups and downs, viewing those elements as part of the wholeness of life has allowed us to build integrated lives of meaning and happiness.

I hope my personal and professional stories will be a source of inspiration, and serve as illustrations of the principles that lead to success. These pages are from my perspective—as a white, cis-gendered male, in a long-term monogamous relationship, with a long history of successful leadership—and thus contain certain biases (which is the case for any personal retrospective).

However, these principles are universal and are not bound by race, gender, sexual orientation, or geography. I believe these principles are adaptable to each individual's unique context. We will explore them in depth in the following chapters:

Chapter 1: Three Key Personal Traits—Commitment, Compassion, Curiosity

Chapter 2: Building a Successful Career—Interviewing, Learning on someone else's dime, Finding mentors

Chapter 3: Being Part of Something Bigger than Yourself—Volunteering to lead, Going full-time non-profit, Career and community

Chapter 4: Seeking Equity Ownership—Recognizing opportunity, Running the show, Moving into the big time

Chapter 5: Building a Happy Life—Work, Learning, Leadership, Adolescence, Adventure, Exploration

Chapter 6: Evolving with a Life Partner—Binding yourselves together, Sharing achievements, Ensuring you don't skip the romance, Doing life together

Chapter 7: Finding an Integrated Life—Drifting, The perfect combination, Personal costs

Chapter 8: Looking Ahead—Generational shifts, Artificial intelligence, Diversity and the future of work

Conclusion: Reflections on Principles—Envisioning a new paradigm, Organizational realities, Keeping the saw sharp, The role of the leader, A final word

Are you ready? Let's get to it.

CHAPTER 1

THREE KEY PERSONAL TRAITS

My parents weren't wealthy when I was growing up, but what they gave to my siblings and me has been more valuable than any monetary boost they might have provided. Dad was a college president, and my mother was his partner. They were both highly intelligent, extraordinarily well-educated, deeply well-mannered, politically aware, religiously faithful, compassionate to individuals, and committed to the community.

All of these traits and priorities were passed on to me, along with good genes that have sustained my health, given me modest athletic ability, and provided a voice and physical presence that can dominate a small gathering or capture an auditorium full of listeners.

My parents' expectations for their four children were that we would behave well, especially around adults. Behaving well did not simply mean that we were silent, but rather that we all learned to engage in meaningful conversation, welcome strangers into a gathering, inquire with interest about another person, and be respectful of all people.

Frank's parents at Davidson College

We were also exposed to people of great intellect and influence. Every sitting governor of North Carolina came to our house to call on Dad. Guests included secretary of state Dean Rusk, senator Terry Sanford, Watergate prosecutor Archibald Cox, and philanthropist E. H. Little. So, I became accustomed to engaging powerful people as the caring human beings they were.

Our parents insisted that we all attend top colleges (we were all good students). As the youngest, I can assure you that they were glad when I won a full scholarship for my four years of undergraduate education. Graduate school was left for me to figure out on my own.

So, I came from a place of privilege, if not great wealth. I am able-bodied, grew up white in the South, was a high school varsity athlete, and was offered the finest in education. But the principles this book will discuss are not about capitalizing on a head start. Rather, what I hope to impart are the foundations that allow anyone to build a successful career and a happy life.

A lot has been written about happiness. In the Presbyterian Church (USA), we talk about four principal areas of wholeness/wellness: spiritual, vocational, financial, and health (physical and mental). I believe all are necessary for true happiness.

Research from Fidelity Investments shows that the single greatest happiness-inducing event in Americans' lives is paying off debt. This exceeds getting married, becoming a parent, getting a raise, or anything else we associate with positive feelings. I still have my canceled loan document from graduate school forty years ago. Paying off that debt was a milestone for Melanie and me.

As I contemplate what leads to meaning and happiness in our lives, I am convinced that positive outcomes in each of the four areas identified by the church are driven by three personal traits.

Commitment, Compassion, Curiosity

In all aspects of your life, three elements must be present and working together to achieve the positive results we all seek. Your **commitment** to excellence in everything you do makes you a valuable partner in relationships. Your **compassion** for others will lead you to a life of hospitality, exhibited in every setting. Your **curiosity** is the basis of learning and developing broad perspectives that will allow you to gain understanding, and ultimately to envision a fulfilling future.

Relationships are supported by each of these personal traits, and it is hard to overstate the importance of those relationships. The Harvard Study of Adult Development finds:

> *"The people who were happiest, who stayed healthiest as they grew old, and who lived the longest were the people who had the warmest connections with other people. In fact, good relationships were the strongest predictor of who was going to be happy and healthy as they grew old."*

When you think about it, commitment, compassion, and curiosity are the elements that bring forth success in all areas of life.

If you want a successful marriage, you have to commit to the other person. You have to care about their feelings and well-being. You have to be constantly curious about what makes them tick, what they want, and what they value, because all of those can change over time.

If you want to be healthy, or go further and be a successful athlete, you have to commit to nutrition, conditioning, and practice. You have to care about others who are on your team or who train with you—athletes tell us over and over that they play harder for their teammates than for themselves, and I have experienced this directly. And you have to be curious and learn how to get better.

If you want a deep spiritual life, you have to commit to a tradition. Untethered spirituality does not lead to deep relationships and deep meaning. Every religious tradition requires that we actively care about what happens to other people who share this earthly plane with us. It is important to question your own tradition as the basis of learning, and be curious as to how others have thought about the essential elements of our existence. As I came to understand my own tradition more deeply through my seminary studies, I became receptive to learning more about other traditions and grew more ecumenical in my perspectives.

If you want to succeed in your career, you have to commit to learning a craft or skill that makes you valuable to your company, customers, or clientele. You have to commit to getting better and staying current, then sharing your expertise for the benefit of your company and colleagues. You have to care about what happens to everyone with whom you enter into transactions. Playing the zero-sum game, where there is one loser and one winner, is destructive beyond a purely short-term horizon, because you become untrustworthy in your circle and in your community.

My work has often called on financial skills, whether as a volunteer developing budgets, grant applications, and financial structures to build affordable housing, or in my paid roles, from reimagining the finances of Habitat for Humanity Charlotte to my current role leading the Board of Pensions of the Presbyterian Church (USA), with over $13 billion in assets and 65,000 beneficiaries.

On three separate occasions, my entire enterprise has teetered on the brink of disaster. In all three cases, the issue was either debt we needed, or debt we doubted we could repay. In a capital-intensive business such as real estate, debt is essential to profitability, but it cuts like a knife when things move against you. In all three cases, my personal relationships saved the day.

Developing skills and relationships across the full spectrum of endeavor will take you places you never could have imagined.

My business pursuits have brought me into meaningful conversations with fascinating people like George H. W. Bush, Colin Powell, the legendary financier Lewis Ranieri, Bart Starr, the infamous former CEO of HealthSouth Richard Scrushy, former Bank of America (B of A) CEO Hugh McColl, Harvard Business School professor Michael Porter, former Augusta National Golf Club chair Billy Payne, Harvard professor and former dean of London Business School John Quelch, investor Roger Ibbotson, and even Sarah Ferguson, Duchess of York.

Melanie and I have been deeply engaged in our communities, including caring ministries and electoral politics. This work has brought us into equally compelling relationships. Melanie and I chatted with President and Mrs. Carter at his boyhood home through Habitat for Humanity. I formed a relationship with Rep. John Lewis of Georgia when serving as chair of Montreat Conference Center. And, thanks to our daughter's relationships, we danced at President Obama's inaugural ball in 2008.

On a Chamber of Commerce inter-city visit, I went bar hopping in Atlanta with soon-to-be governor of North Carolina, Pat McCrory. McCrory's successor was governor Roy Cooper, a longtime friend and fraternity brother. We have visited the home of former White House chief of staff Erskine Bowles while working on Democratic campaigns. And most recently, we were invited to participate in Renaissance Weekend, developed and led by former US ambassador Phil Lader and his wife, Linda.

At other times, engagement has tested my character. Representing Habitat for Humanity, I was called to Congress by Rep. Shelley Capito to testify in relation to mortgage rules and the origins of the global financial crisis of 2008. When I refused to acknowledge the Dodd-Frank bill as a plausible fix to the circumstances that plunged the world into financial turmoil, I became the subject of intense scrutiny. It's no fun taking angry calls from congressional offices. Ultimately, I was pushed into defending my position on the national editorial pages of the McClatchy newspapers.

Melanie and I have been active in the Presbyterian Church, where I am now an ordained minister of Word and Sacrament. We have served as youth advisors, teachers, coaches, and hosts for our unhoused neighbors on Monday nights, always working together.

Everyone can build a life of meaning and happiness. Whether you are still in school, early in your career, or guiding your own children, these principles will serve you well.

Robert Waldinger, the director of the Harvard Study of Adult Development, says:

> *"I've heard people in their twenties and certainly older say, 'It's too late for me. I'm not good at relationships. It's never going to happen for me. I give up.' We had people in our study who gave up, and then, when they least expected it, new stuff happened... I want to leave people with the fact that, at least from our data, if you think you know it's too late for you, think again: you don't know."*

No matter where you are now, you can make a decision to either keep going or change course. Finding your north star, the thing to which you are truly committed, is the key. Think about the nature of navigating your course. No matter how long you have been wandering or where you find yourself at this moment, you can get out your compass and your very next step can be toward the true north.

Let's get going.

CHAPTER 2

BUILDING A SUCCESSFUL CAREER

Every successful career has to have a beginning, a time for developing expertise, and then an expansion of responsibilities that results in a true leadership opportunity. But it all starts with the interview process. Whether you are coming out of college, graduate school, or simply looking for the entry point to a new direction in your career, you will need to interview. So, let's start there.

Interviewing

I stood in the placement office chatting with the attendant at the counter. She had just told me that Mr. Steele Alphin, the bank officer with whom I wanted to interview, had not listed German majors as eligible to sign up. Apparently, he was looking for economics, business, and accounting.

I read his interview schedule upside down as I kept the attendant talking long enough to memorize where he would be. Reading upside down across a desk is a skill that has served me well in many instances, including obtaining our first apartment at Harvard Business School. Thanks to this trick, I learned that Mr. Alphin was interviewing in room 107 of Phillips Hall, and was scheduled for a break from 12:30 to 2 p.m.

As 12:30 approached, I waited down the hall, resume in hand. Mr. Alphin emerged and quickly headed for the door to the outside. I followed. He walked across campus, heading for downtown Franklin Street. I kept back, my target always in sight. He crossed and went into the local bank branch.

Through the window, I saw him slide in behind one of the desks in the little business cubes that filled the local branches in the early 1980s. I waited three minutes, and then walked straight to the teller line. "I'm here to see Mr. Alphin," I said confidently. The teller answered, "He's right over there. Just go over and let him know you are here."

I walked to the cube. "Excuse me, Mr. Alphin. I'm Frank Spencer, and I couldn't sign up for an interview because my major wasn't on your list. I'm a German major, speak and read French and Spanish, and placed out of calculus as a freshman." I didn't let him get a word in as I continued, "I'm a Morehead scholar from Charlotte-Mecklenburg Schools. Here is my resume. As I understand it, NCNB is dramatically expanding its international banking business. Could we talk about my interest in being a part of your Management Associates Program?"

I had done my homework. I called him by name. I

connected to his hometown. We began a conversation that resulted in an invitation to come to Charlotte for additional interviews. A few weeks later, I had a job offer.

As I began interviewing for jobs coming out of business school four years later, I came to believe in a fatalistic approach to the whole process. I believe all professional opportunities are mutual discernment experiences, in which the potential employer is trying to decide if you are the right fit and, equally importantly, where you as well are determining if the organization is the right fit for you.

In my last semester of business school, I interviewed with twenty-seven companies and got seven offers. Twenty companies assessed what I brought to the table and said, "No thanks." I was not accustomed to being turned down, and had to adjust my expectations. You have to be totally honest for this process to work, and recognize that there will be more declines than offers.

I shifted my focus to the two areas where I had the most interest, real estate and consulting. Both of these fields are project-based rather than process-oriented. There are many people who derive great satisfaction from incrementally improving a repeating process, but I am not one of them. I need to see through the completion of a complex but finite project, even if the time horizon is measured in years.

I had an offer from Bain & Company, the high-flying consulting firm where I had interned in the summer of 1985. At that time, they were exceedingly proud of working for only one company in each industry, and tracked "the Bain portfolio," showing how their clients outperformed the market. They were making so much money, the partners decided to create Bain Capital to invest in their own buyouts and turnarounds. Mitt Romney was given the task of standing up the new company.

I knew Bain wasn't right for us. I had attended dinners that were being charged to clients where we wagered on how high the bill would be for team members with no clients present. During an internal orientation on the project to which I was being assigned, the partner in charge made fun of the names of managers at the North Carolina company where we were hired to develop strategy. One of those names was my wife's uncle, Crash Davis. Two years later, a film producer called Uncle Crash and asked to use his name for the movie *Bull Durham*.

Finally, at a summer dinner, one of the senior partners hit on Melanie. Although Bain was the most money on the table for us at the time, we knew it wasn't the place for us.

A stranger opportunity arose with Mark Twain Bancshares. In one of my management classes, we had studied a case on their unique branch-based structure in which each physical branch was its own corporation, which was mandated by the state of Missouri in response to the Great Depression.

I signed up to meet Adam Aaronson, the company's CEO. On the spot, he offered me the position of bank president for one of their largest Kansas City branches. I equivocated and said I needed to talk to Melanie about the potential of moving to Missouri, and I noted that she was an accomplished banker and marketer in her own right.

He asked if she was on campus, and interviewed her that day. She was offered the bank president role at another of the company's branches. While this was flattering and intriguing, we agreed that evening to pass. Anyone with the power to create presidents on the spot could just as easily withdraw favor without warning. We were looking for something more substantial.

I had not been interested in investment banks, having kept my interviewing mostly to real estate and consulting. We knew we didn't want to live in New York City, and the business process itself was unappealing. When Raymond James came to campus in the I-banking group, I initially passed the opportunity by. However, when I heard from friends that they were based in St. Petersburg, Florida, were focused on real estate, and had a very different approach in dealing with retail customers rather than institutions, I decided to make a pitch. I hurried to the office they were using for interviews, resume in hand. I made my case as the interviewer was packing up, and he agreed to take a look and be in touch.

I was one of five candidates they chose to fly down to Florida for final interviews. At one point, each of us sat alone in Bo Godbold's office, and he asked the same question:

"If we extend an offer, what are the chances you will accept?"

"Forty percent," was my response.

"Forty percent?" Bo said with disbelief.

I continued, "I really like you guys and how you approach your business, but this would be my seventh offer. At forty percent, I would put you in the lead."

Upon returning to the hotel where we were all staying, we of course compared notes. All four of my classmates had answered Bo's question with an enthusiastic "100 percent." My honesty prevailed. I was offered the job later that week, and ultimately decided to turn it down. But I had forged a friendship that would last long into my career. Nineteen years later, when I took my company public, Raymond James was a part of the stock distribution team, and their analysts faithfully covered us for our entire existence.

Learning on someone else's dime

My parents gave me many things in terms of life skills, education, and perspective, but capital to start a business was not something they could provide. I had been on scholarships throughout college, and worked to get my spending money. My convenient but low-wage work at the University of North Carolina was as a waiter at my own fraternity house. We ate together every evening. I figured if the brothers wanted to pay me in the form of a reduced monthly bill, I didn't mind handing out the full dishes and doing the washing up afterwards.

But my real money came driving for Domino's Pizza. The Chapel Hill store was the third-busiest in the national chain, which, by 1981, had grown to 500 stores. There were multiple sources of income. We worked an eight- to ten-hour shift and got paid minimum wage.

Because we drove our own cars, we got eight to ten percent of total delivery earnings for mileage. We got an extra two percent for being high driver of the shift, and a one-percent bonus if our bank balanced to the penny. All that plus tips.

I drove Tuesdays and Saturdays. On a big night, I could clear $200, only $33.45 of which appeared on my

W-2. I routinely pocketed over $300 a week during the semester, giving me plenty for dates, entertainment, gas, and beer. There is nothing like working hard and having your own money to spend.

When I took the job at North Carolina National Bank (NCNB), my $17,000 salary was substantially below the $20 per hour I often netted at Domino's. But compensation notwithstanding, it was an amazing learning experience. I started in the credit department in August, after returning from ten weeks of study and travel on the borders of France, compliments of my Morehead Scholarship.

We all started in the credit department. We learned to "spread" the financial statements of companies in the way the bank wanted to underwrite loans. Within six months, my innate math skills, and the fact that I was the only one in the department who could read the majority of the European financial statements, brought me a promotion to senior international credit reviewer for NCNB. With a new crop of management associates due in a few months, my salary was increased to $19,500. Still not as much as pizza delivery, but headed in the right direction.

Part of being in the credit department was going to credit school. We were taught finance and underwriting in the real world using the actual files of bank customers. At age twenty-two, I was managing a team of analysts. I worked side by side with a senior officer on the bank's largest delinquent loan, which had been originated in our nascent Hong Kong office. I spread the financial statements of every European corresponding bank. At just short of a year on the job, I got moved upstairs.

I joined the European area as an international banking representative. I was responsible for the European bank portfolio, and began trading banker's acceptances for our European customers. I would finance their letters of credit at a spread of twenty-five to thirty basis points above our cost, and then go over to our Asian area where a colleague would get the transaction guaranteed by paying a Japanese bank ten basis points.

The Federal Reserve had given us a ruling that any transaction guaranteed by a bank with assets over $1 billion could be taken off our liabilities and deducted from our capital reserve requirements. Thus, my department was making fifteen to twenty basis points on each transaction. I could do approximately one of these transactions per quarter with each European bank.

I built the portfolio to a notional amount of almost $90 million, or about $150,000 of annual profit with zero invested capital, and therefore an infinite return on investment. My boss thought I was a genius, since his bonus was based on total return on investment and my portfolio increased the numerator without increasing the denominator.

The bank's chief credit officer did not agree. As I sat at the end of the long table, trying to explain to the credit committee of senior executives why my portfolio had no risk and an even better return, J. W. Smith, with his face set sternly at the other end of the table, simply pointed out that while the Fed may have ruled one way, the outstanding balances I had booked exceeded every approved credit line by a factor of at least double.

My creativity squashed, and acutely aware that the newly minted MBA who I was teaching was making more than twice what I was, I decided to return to business school. But I had learned a great deal. I understood bank underwriting in a variety of industries. The bank had taught me accounting and basic finance. I had managed people and been responsible for group outcomes. Perhaps most importantly, I had learned that large institutions may value their policies and strictures over creativity.

It was hard to see how far I had come in just two years until I met a comparison group at Harvard Business School. My section of ninety people had eight CPAs and a dozen former investment banking analysts. When we took diagnostic tests in accounting and finance in the first couple weeks of school, I placed in the top five of the class. I had already developed mastery of key financial concepts.

I certainly hadn't learned that stuff in German class. I learned it all at the bank. Ever since, whenever a young person asks about a career, I always push them toward a large, well-capitalized institution with a robust training program. Those types of organizations will expose you to a much greater deal volume and variety than small enterprises. Friends who went small, thinking they would gain experience in a wider variety of tasks, never really caught up. It is even worse if you go directly into the non-profit world.

Coming out of business school, the offer I had from McKinsey & Company to join their Atlanta office in management consulting was very tempting. McKinsey focused on disseminating best practices across industries rather than being hyper-competitive within a single industry, the way Bain did.

The starting salary was $65,000 base with a $15,000 annual bonus and $15,000 to sign on. But the job would require traveling four to five days per week, and spouses were expected to be at home as support. With a spouse who was destined for much more than permanent support, and with a toddler at home, Melanie and I moved in a different direction. Little did we know that toddler would grow up to become a Baker Scholar at HBS and, ultimately, a McKinsey partner.

I took a job with a large regional real estate company. At $36,000, it was the lowest-paying of my seven offers but promised the most access to real deal flow and proximity to family and friends. I started as an assistant project manager while most other real estate companies saw me as an analyst or junior broker. I had lots of business-school skills, and was the only person in the company with a personal computer on their desk in 1986.

However, I could not read blueprints, and so immediately enrolled at the community college for night classes in construction estimating. I then enrolled in real estate classes and passed my state brokerage exam, bypassing the sales designation and going straight to the top classification. In my first year, I had added a key skill and attained my professional license.

I began project development as an apprentice. For the first few months, I went with my boss, Jim Merrifield, to all of his meetings. We met with architects, contractors, sub-contractors, potential tenants, attorneys, bankers, city officials—all the people who are necessary to any development project.

He always gave me my own set of plans, whether for grading and road construction in a 200-acre business park, or for a flex-space building for distribution and light manufacturing. He expected me to mark them up with my own questions and comments. I discovered I could focus on those two-dimensional drawings and transport myself into the three-dimensional space, looking around at what would be, able to see strange roof configurations or conflicts between duct work and structural joists.

The next step was a shift in leadership. We still attended all the same meetings, but now I ran them as he observed. He would give me periodic critiques on my project leadership skills. After several months of this new pattern, Jim told me he would no longer attend my meetings, and he assigned me half of the projects we had going. I only needed to check back with him if I felt unsure about a decision.

A year and a half into my tenure, a very large public-private venture with the city came our way. It was financially, structurally, and legally very complex. As the only executive who had a computer, I was immediately pulled into the planning and negotiating. I did all of the financial modeling, and we signed the deal. I was named the project manager on what would become the largest project our company had ever undertaken.

The whole thing was very high-profile, and I found myself in the mayor's office, the editor's office at the newspaper, and meeting with the president of the bank I had left four years earlier. When then–vice president George H. W. Bush signed on to be the keynote speaker at the groundbreaking, the political advance teams and Secret Service ran me ragged. They insisted that I get a high school band to greet the VP. I called every school in the county, but it was the first week of June and all the bands had wrapped up for the year. Instead, I arranged for the Voltage Brothers, a local cover band who were playing for the party that night, to come early and provide music.

As word of our special guest spread, local politicians and business leaders wanted to get on the stage. My six-chair stage now extended to include over twenty additional seats, as well as a platform for the Voltage Brothers. I stood backstage with George H. W. Bush, and my voice boomed through the mic, asking the crowd to welcome the Vice President of the United States. The Voltage Brothers took their cue and began playing James Brown's "Living in America." Just before I guided the vice president through the curtain, I told him to turn left, toward his chair.

Of course, the person to the right stuck out his hand for a shake, and what politician could resist that? Each of the twenty to the right in turn extended a hand, and Bush worked his way down the entire the line while the Voltage Brothers jammed. He got to the end of the row, and, finding no chair, turned around and made his way back to the main part of the stage where the mayor and our congressional delegation waited.

The event was front-page news. Over 1,200 people attended that night. Eighteen months later, the grand opening was such a big deal that I hired the Temptations as the evening's entertainment.

Leading such a high-profile project took every skill I had learned up to that point. But the skills I brought were not my most powerful tools. Rather, I discovered a phrase that has become my magic words: "I don't know how that works. Please explain it to me."

Pretending to understand a complex issue in order to get through a meeting without embarrassment is a fool's bargain. Having the confidence to admit you don't know opens the door to actual learning.

I went to the construction site almost every day. I would ask the superintendent to explain what he was looking for as we walked the 400,000-square-foot structure. The project architect taught me how to inspect the work for quality. I thought the mason's head would explode the day the architect pulled the newly laid brick off the wall when he discovered a sloppy application. The structural engineer showed me how the "moments of stress" are calculated. Each of the subs taught me as well. I learned about plumbing, wiring, and HVAC (heating, ventilation, and air conditioning). I even learned how to bend rebar and pour concrete, and what kind of coating you need to go on it. I got this education by simply asking how things work.

I did the leasing for the building. We added a hotel with a rooftop pool. I learned how parking decks work, and what leads to profits or losses when running them. We overcame easement issues with the adjacent railroad. We executed a ground lease with the city and an air rights lease with the hotel. I negotiated the mortgage for the building and the city's contribution. All completed on time and within budget, a year of planning and eighteen months of construction.

Four and a half years into my real estate career, I was promoted to vice president and moved to our multi-family division. But I was getting restless, not sure I was in the right place.

Five years earlier, I had graduated from Harvard Business School as a Baker Scholar. They asked all of us to consider applying for the Dean's Fellowship, a full ride to complete a PhD and become a professor. Professor Michael Porter had been my teacher for industry and competitive analysis, and had invited me to assist him on his book, *The Competitive Advantage of Nations*. It was tempting, but our family wanted to get back to North Carolina, and so I declined the offer.

The option was open for five years, and I was in the last year of that cycle. I talked with John Quelch, my marketing professor from five years back, and he encouraged me to apply. I made it to the final group and was flown to Boston for an interview. When asked about my research interest, I said I was interested in developing a model for ethical corporate decision-making. I left feeling good.

A call from the dean two weeks later dashed my hopes. He said that the committee liked me and thought that I had great promise as a teacher, but they had polled the faculty and no one was willing to support my research topic. The answer was no.

I was ahead of my time. Within five years, HBS was fully entrenched in attempts to define and research integrity and ethics. The 1980s' decade of greed had given way to the decade of community responsibility and shared values. In retrospect, it was the best decision for both of us.

I rededicated myself to my work in real estate, determined to create meaning in the projects I took on. I built high-density apartments in some locations and led the process for affordable housing, using Low-Income

Housing Tax Credits, in others. After two years of developing apartments, I was made corporate vice president for marketing and strategy across the whole organization: commercial, retail, residential, land development, and construction.

On my sixth anniversary, my pay package equaled the McKinsey starting offer, plus three percent ownership in the projects I developed.

After two years at the bank, two years in business school, and seven years in real estate, my mastery had developed across a full range of skills: underwriting, lending, finance, marketing, brokerage, construction, development, and all of the associated legal requirements. I was thirty-two years old. At no point in that journey was my own capital at risk. The entire time, someone else had been paying me to become an expert.

Finding mentors

There's been an overabundance of advice concerning mentors published recently. Most of it is pure folly. Here are instructions that are typical of current thinking, compliments of Google:

- Reflect on your goals and needs for mentorship.

- Consider people you admire and who have the skills or experience you want to gain.

- Start with your network and reach out to potential mentors via email, social media, or phone.

- Ask for an initial conversation to get to know them and see if they are a good fit.

- Formalize the relationship, and structure your mentorship with clear expectations and goals.

The only part of this with which I agree is constantly considering and updating your personal goals. This is a discipline which I have followed throughout my career, particularly at critical junctures of change. But the idea that you ask someone to be your mentor or formalize the relationship in writing is a terrible idea. I have been mentored and, in turn, mentored dozens of people in both for-profit and non-profit settings. In all cases, the relationships were organic, whether I was the one learning or the one guiding.

I have had two great mentors in my professional career. These are the true relationships that last.

The first person I considered a mentor was Hugh McColl. When I came to NCNB, Hugh was number two at a regional bank that had aspirations of international significance, but a footprint limited to North Carolina by interstate banking laws. At the zenith of his career, Mr. McColl was CEO of Bank of America, which his bank NCNB, and then NationsBank, had purchased. His vision led Charlotte to become the second-largest banking center in the United States, trailing only New York City.

My earliest encounters with Mr. McColl were in credit school, where he taught lending. I still remember his admonition, "Never let a good deal get away because of tight pricing, and never do a bad deal because of wide margins." His point, which I have applied throughout my career, is that the right deals with the right people will always pay off, but going for the big score with the wrong people or via a shaky deal will sink you.

Our relationship grew naturally. The credit department members would often go for beers in the first-floor deli on Friday afternoons, and Mr. McColl would sometimes join his young colleagues there. I made it a point to be there. It was Hugh McColl who said to me one day, "Frank, I am the last person without a graduate degree who will be CEO of a major bank." I decided that day I would eventually go back for a master's degree, whether or not I stayed in banking, or decided to try something else.

Although he loved to promote his ex-Marine tough-guy persona, Hugh is one of the most compassionate people I have known. While I was serving as senior international credit reviewer, a young man from our London office came to spend some time in my department. Shortly after arriving, he found himself in the emergency room, admitted to the hospital, and diagnosed with cancer. He knew no one in this country but his work colleagues, and I became the focal point for his care.

Every other day, Hugh would call me or drop by my desk. "Tell me how Richard's doing," he would say in his clipped Carolina accent, with no introduction or explanation. I would give a report, and he would tell me to call every other day if I didn't see him.

Each time I called Mr. McColl, now the bank CEO, he answered his own phone, "NCNB, Hugh McColl." In fact, he was a fanatic about it. I picked up the habit, and never had assistants screen my calls. To this day, I still send out my direct phone number on every letter and email, and I return every call and answer every piece of correspondence.

Hugh McColl

It turned out that Richard needed surgery. Mr. McColl arranged for his father to fly over and stay at the bank's expense until Richard was well enough to travel home.

My relationship with Hugh didn't stop at the office door. He was deeply involved in local Democratic politics, and as Melanie and I volunteered and captained numerous precincts our paths often crossed outside of work. After returning to Charlotte from Boston, Melanie and I gave modestly (we were mostly broke), but still made a point of attending political events where we almost always ran into Mr. McColl.

When my company began work on the large public-private real estate venture for which I was named project manager, it was Hugh McColl's office in which I found myself negotiating the loan from NCNB. He now saw me in a different light as our paths continued to cross in civic, political, and business venues. Though not appointed by Mr. McColl, I was asked to serve on the first business advisory board for the newly created McColl School of Business at Queens University. That brought us together once again.

One of the most fun experiences I associate with Mr. McColl was at a Carolina Panthers football game. In January of 1997, I was invited to the bank's box for the Panthers' first playoff game against the Dallas Cowboys. Our loan officer was way down on the priority list and so had put his name on the potential, but unlikely, playoff game at the start of the 1996 season. When the Panthers won their division, they hosted the wild-card Cowboys. There was Hugh, wearing his Panthers do-rag, leaning out of the open box window, leading the cheers. As the Panthers cruised to victory, there were hugs and high fives all around.

It was this same bank, now Bank of America, that became the primary lender and co-book runner for the company I would take public fifteen years later. Hugh McColl had a tremendous influence on my professional career throughout our relationship, but he probably wouldn't say, "I was Frank's first mentor."

The second mentor that shaped me professionally was John Crosland, owner of the real estate company where I began work right out of business school. At first, I rarely saw him. I had been hired into a new small subsidiary focusing on commercial real estate. I was the first project manager in the commercial division.

It was quite a while before I realized that we were one of the smaller pieces of the Crosland enterprise. The biggest part was the home-building company. When I arrived in 1986, John was already entertaining discussions about selling the business, which his father had started and which had delivered 10,000 single-family houses. In fact, John had recently been named US home builder of the year.

The home-building company sold nine days before the stock market crash of 1987, at a very handsome price. That gave the Crosland family substantial liquid capital and allowed John to turn his attention to his other interests.

John was a big believer in professional development. As I was being promoted to project manager, I was likewise told that I had to attend a series of training sessions in Atlanta that were mandatory for all managers in John's orbit. We learned recruiting, talent management, and goal-setting. Every manager was expected to use these skills.

John was a demanding leader. The sign behind his desk read:

Do it all.
Do it all right.
Do it all right now.

His drive for excellence reinforced my own self-motivation toward achievement. I started to get noticed more and more by our leader. First, I was developing the largest project that the company had undertaken, and the family equity investment was in the millions. John enjoyed being on the front page of the paper with Vice President Bush.

I was the first vice president to transfer between companies, a generalist in a world of specialists. After I had brought in all my projects on time and within budget, John asked me to fill the newly created role of corporate vice president for marketing and strategy. All of a sudden, I was in every executive meeting with the company presidents, the CFO, and John.

As my direct work with John Crosland expanded, we had an opportunity to acquire a failed savings and loan (S&L) association in North Carolina. The S&L crisis had begun in 1986. By 1989, the Resolution Trust Corporation (RTC) had been formed and began "selling" S&Ls. In

John Crosland

the early 1990s, the pace greatly accelerated through a bizarre bidding process. Bidders would say how much the RTC must pay for the bidder to take the organization. John had me analyze every loan in the target portfolio, and our bid was negative $400 million. John then decided we needed to go to New York to find a backer.

We entered the offices of Hyperion Partners on a crisp fall afternoon. Our meeting was with founder Lewis Ranieri. Ranieri had been vice chairman of Salomon Brothers and is widely credited with the creation of mortgage-backed securities, as detailed in the Michael Lewis book *Liar's Poker*. Ranieri and Crosland had served on the National Housing Council together.

"Louie," as John greeted him, sat behind a huge desk. A short, heavyset man with days-old stubble all over his cheeks and neck, chewing an unlit cigar, he looked more like an unkempt teddy bear than one of the top financiers in the world. We made the pitch for our $400 million S&L. Louie responded with the gravel of too many cigars and scotches seasoning his voice. He lifted his hand right below his chin and said, "John, you know I love you, baby, but I am up to here buying one of my own in Texas. I just can't be distracted by a small deal in North Carolina." A few more niceties and the meeting was over. We did not win the subsequent bid.

However, Hyperion bought Bank United of Texas at a total transaction cost of around $3 billion. They would later sell the same institution to investors for $18 billion. Michael Lewis would again profile Ranieri in the book *The Big Short*. What I learned is that entrepreneurs will rise and fall, but the people who control capital transactions almost always win, coming and going.

Like Hugh McColl, John never dodged interactions with his customers. Many home builders don't want the people who buy their homes to be able to contact them, but John never had an unlisted number. Despite home warranties lasting only one year by statute, if a homeowner called, John would send our construction team out to inspect and repair if needed, even fifteen years after the home sale and six years after he had sold the company. He felt it was his reputation on the line.

As much as I learned directly from John—about reading research, diligence, excellence, service, and the importance of reputation—it was as I was leaving that he taught me the greatest lesson. I had been restless with the knowledge that the five company presidents were all in their late thirties or forties, which led to a growing sense that I needed to do something bigger for the community.

I found myself one of two finalists to become the first executive director of the Children's Services Network (CSN), a five-party collaboration between the city, county, school system, United Way, and Chamber of Commerce. Its mission was to coordinate and rationalize all services for children, from age zero to eighteen, in Charlotte and Mecklenburg County. As a quasi-public entity, the board decided that finalist interviews would be conducted in public, and the local newspaper was going to run a front-page profile on the two candidates the next morning.

I went into John's office and said, "Um, there's going to be something in the paper tomorrow that I want to tell you in advance." I told John the whole story. Some bosses would have said, "If you're not committed to this business, just pack up now." Instead, John said to me, "Frank, if this is something that you feel will benefit our community, then you have my full support. I feel confident that you will be selected, but if you are not, know you always have a place here." He went on to say that should I win, I must ensure they allow me to do consulting on the side.

What I was doing would not affect John's lifestyle nor the outcomes for his business, and he wanted the best for everyone who worked with him and for the community at large. I have tried to emulate that same perspective throughout my life and career.

That kind of attitude won John fierce loyalty from his many professional colleagues. It is said in Charlotte that if you ever worked for John Crosland, you always work for John Crosland. That is true. I did win the job, and he immediately hired me as his strategy and succession-planning consultant. I served as an investment committee member for his daughter's trust. He had me represent him in selecting the John Crosland Professor of Real Estate at UNC Charlotte, and then serve on the new program's board of advisors.

Two years after he died, John's personal attorney called me out of the blue. She said that John had left a substantial amount to create the Crosland Charitable Foundation and that he had pre-selected an approved slate of trustees. My name was on the list, and she asked if I would serve if elected. Of course, I said yes.

Hugh McColl and John Crosland had an intersection that was also important in my life, as they were two of the founding board members of Habitat for Humanity Charlotte. John chaired the board, and I later discovered that he was the source of an annual anonymous gift that magically balanced the budget in the early years. Mr. McColl drove NCNB/NationsBank/Bank of America to become a top donor and volunteer source for Habitat nationwide. His retirement gift from his colleagues was 100 homes built in his honor.

These two men brought President and Mrs. Carter to Charlotte for the first-ever Carter Work Project in 1987. That's where I first met the former president and when I began my lifelong work with Habitat, which would culminate in my becoming president of Habitat Charlotte.

The Spencers with President and Mrs. Carter

I found myself sitting once again in John's living room near the end of his life, as he continued as one of Habitat's major donors. His last words to me, squeezed out through a body racked with Parkinson's disease, were, "I should have never let you go. You were to be my successor."

CHAPTER 3

BEING PART OF SOMETHING BIGGER THAN YOURSELF

Building a happy and meaningful life can't be limited to your profession and your family, even though both of those are critical components. You have to find a way to be a part of something bigger than yourself. The same principles of commitment, compassion, and curiosity apply in both civic life and in your faith community. You must commit to those issues which are important to you. You will find fulfillment when you work with compassion for the good of others. If you allow yourself to be curious, without judgment, you will find that you can learn about people who have lived experiences that are very different from your own.

For me, that has always been both the community in which we live and the church in which we worship, teach, and lead. Each brings a different aspect of meaning to life, and often, I have found that the two intersect.

Volunteering to lead

Right out of college, Melanie and I were both working for NCNB. The corporate expectation in Charlotte was that professionals would also engage with the community. We volunteered as youth advisors at our church, and also did our share of projects at the bank, like hosting the local golf tournament or volunteering for United Way.

During the two years between college and graduate school, we were Democratic precinct captains. We signed on to D. G. Martin's bid for Congress. It was an open seat, and we were devastated when our candidate came up less than 400 votes short.

We returned to Charlotte after graduate school and immediately began working on D. G.'s second attempt to win a congressional seat. It was a rematch, but this time the opponent was the incumbent. Our candidate lost again, by an even wider margin. Having experienced disappointment in more than one political campaign, I turned my energies toward other forms of civic engagement.

My first major community role was as the vice chair of the board of the Transitional Families Program at the Charlotte Housing Authority. The basic concept was to fix participants' rent at thirty percent of gross income (a federal requirement), and, over the next five to seven years, provide case management services to help with education, employment opportunities, and ultimately increased income.

As wages increased, so did rent. However, all funds above the rent amount at the beginning of the program were set aside in a savings account, which the participant would eventually use to move to private sector housing. I brought in Melanie, now an expert in market research, to conduct focus groups that helped us shape the program.

The escrowing of the savings required an act of Congress for authority, and we got great help from our local representative, Alec McMillan, to get it through. It took four years to get the first family into private sector housing, but by the end of the fifth year we were moving one family every week.

The Clinton administration was so enamored of what we accomplished that our program became the basis of their "Ending Welfare as We Know It" legislation. However, I thought that they were misreading the results. Our program focused on those near the top of the capability scale and helped them get past barriers to private housing; it was never aimed at all residents. The Clinton administration made the mistake of applying these principles to everyone receiving assistance, with often dire consequences for those who could not work their way out of welfare.

In 1990, we were back in the throes of politics. The mayor of Charlotte, who had engaged with me on the public-private venture, was Harvey Gantt. He was running as the Democratic nominee for Senate against incumbent Jesse Helms. This contest is famously remembered for the ad in which a pair of white hands crumpled a rejection letter based on quotas. In a bitter, racially charged contest, Helms was re-elected, our hard work again having produced no results. However, civic relationships continued to grow.

With John Crosland's encouragement, I had gone through the Chamber of Commerce Leadership School, a program designed to encourage civic engagement. In 1992, the Charlotte-Mecklenburg Schools asked the chamber to undertake an operational review of the non-instructional components of its organization.

I chaired the Organizational Analysis Subcommittee. Our task was to integrate all other studies (transportation, food service, facilities, HR, finance, security) into one coherent strategic plan. My role had me in regular conversation with the superintendent and presenting to the school board in public meetings.

During the first seven years after business school, my involvement with the church grew alongside my professional career and community engagement. I taught adult Sunday school, was elected deacon and then elder, founded the housing ministry, and was asked to serve on the New Horizons Campaign, the first capital campaign in a decade and the first to ask for commitments of time as well as treasure. Joining me on that committee was the CEO of Duke Power, soon to become Duke Energy.

For our family, the most meaningful work through the church was a program called Wonderful Wednesdays. This program provided faith formation and a meal to the children of Piedmont Courts, part of the Charlotte Housing Authority. It was housed at Seigle Avenue Presbyterian Church and funded by our congregation. Melanie and I taught for seven straight years on every Wednesday evening of the school year. We made great friends who we otherwise would never have met, and were able to provide our children with a window into cultural differences that they otherwise would never have seen.

Seigle Avenue also ran a pre-school during the week for many of those same children. I joined the board of directors, and was immediately made treasurer. It was my first experience running payroll and creating tax forms.

Going full-time non-profit

These currents came together for me as I began to consider leaving real estate to become the first executive director of the Children's Services Network. I was deeply involved in issues of housing, education, and early childhood development. My public roles had made me well known at the Chamber of Commerce, in the mayor's office, at the school board, and among local political and business leaders. As John Crosland suspected, it wasn't a surprise that I was selected to lead this new agency with an impossibly broad mission.

As I prepared to leave the Crosland organization, the head of human resources took me aside and begged me to reconsider. "You're committing career suicide," he said. For me, I really felt that God was calling me to this work. I also had a wife who was fully supportive, for which I am still amazed and thankful. After all, she had put me through business school, scrimped to pay off our debt, and, just as my career was looking productive, I was switching to the non-profit world.

Setting up CSN was an education in itself. I got a small empty office suite from United Way as their contribution to the effort. No furniture, no phone, not even a trash can. Everywhere else I had ever worked, all of those things had been waiting for me. Needless to say, I figured all that out and hired two colleagues, a do-it-all administrative assistant and a PhD researcher. I set up all the payroll and a 403b retirement account, did the books, and began to settle in.

The first project selected by the board of directors was the reduction of teen pregnancy. The year was 1993, and our county's teen pregnancy rate was twenty-five percent higher than the country's as a whole. Our goal was to cut the rate in half, and so "Fifty percent by 2000" became the community focus.

The upside of such an ambitious goal was that I needed to bring the heads of all the major children-serving agencies to the table. I used my financial skills to build a model of how much the community was spending based on each teen pregnancy. Statistics were readily available in many cases, while others were developed in collaboration with the agencies. The data told us that teen pregnancy was costing Mecklenburg County over $33 million a year. From there, we created a comprehensive plan with participation from every agency and CSN's five sponsoring entities.

The plan worked. The programs that were put in place cut the teen pregnancy rate in half by 1998. While we were lucky that national trends were declining over the same period, by 2000 our community's rate was now substantially below the national average.

The other benefit of our collaboration was an ongoing council of executives, which I chaired. We developed a scorecard for the youth of our community, "A Report on the Future." Published annually, it was divided into two foci:

1 Measures for adolescent outcomes: teen pregnancy, youth crime, substance abuse, completion of high school

2 Measures for early childhood: abuse and neglect, low birth weight, school readiness, children in poverty

This work thrust me into the very center of civic life in Charlotte. I was interviewed regularly on TV and radio.

Our reports generated front-page news. I was a part of the budgeting and allocation process for each of my five sponsors. I began to hear politicians and government officials ask, "What will the Children's Services Network say about [insert issue]?" As it turned out, my decision had not been career suicide as predicted. Instead, still in my early thirties, I was seen as a community leader with the skills to bring people together.

My three years leading CSN were not without challenges and detractors. One of the largest agencies serving children focused on preschool education and child care, and its executive director saw our work as a threat to her agency's stranglehold on county funding. It had Commissioner Lloyd Sher on its side, who consistently opposed us in budget hearings. I was never able to bring either of them to our perspective.

Fortunately, Lloyd's was the only vote ever cast against CSN: all other commissioners and city council representatives voted for us. I had worked the Democrats hard, and, with the help of the other agencies, moved the agenda from one focused on funding needs to gaining greater funding for positive outcomes. The Republicans liked my business-school approach to strategy and the accountability of our focus on outcome statistics.

In one memorable budget session, the most conservative member of the County Commission said, "I've never fully understood what Frank and Children's Services Network are trying to do, but if Lloyd is against them, I am sure I am for them." All the Republicans joined the Democrats and voted in the affirmative.

I learned a great deal about myself leading CSN—notably about failings in my leadership style, as I was unable to create complete consensus. Even so, the work was rewarding, but I found that I missed finance and real estate. My limited consulting work and my brokerage license kept me current, but never replaced the excitement of a deal or the satisfaction of seeing a building materialize. I realized that while I was having an impact in the community, there were other people quite capable of leading service coordination for children.

The hand I had been dealt, and had also deliberately chosen, was that I was really good in finance, marketing, strategy, and organizational structure. I realized I could do a lot of good by creating jobs that paid well and developing buildings that were positive for the world. So when my friend, Pahl, sat next to me in continuing education for our real estate licenses and said, "I want to recruit you to be my boss," I was ready to listen.

On January 2, 1996, I joined the Cogdell Group, where I would remain for the next fifteen years, focused on real estate for the healthcare industry.

Career and community

Even though I was taking on a new job and learning a new aspect of the real estate world, I never abandoned civic and church engagement. I went on the board of advisors for the Chamber of Commerce. A year later, I was appointed to the city's Capital Needs Advisory Committee. I had retained my full membership in the Urban Land Institute throughout my time at CSN, and shifted from the National Policy Council to the Corporate Real Estate Council.

At church, I continued to serve as an elder and as the housing ministry chair. In August of 1996, I led a group of fifteen disciples from our church on a seventeen-day Habitat for Humanity mission to Ekwendeni, Malawi. It was in the sanctuary in Ekwendeni that I preached my first sermon, describing my encounter with a homeless man and the lengths we went through to reunite him with his family. It was also where I learned that the phrase "It takes a village to raise a child" actually means the extended family who live near each other, not a community's social services, as Hillary Clinton would later posit.

In the first five years of the new millennium, business was going well and engagement expanded. I became a mentor in the chamber's Minority Business Leaders Institute. I served on the local troop committee and the county executive committee of the Boy Scouts. I became vice chair of my fraternity's foundation. I went on the advisory board of First Citizens Bank and the board of the real estate program at the University of North Carolina in Charlotte, where I also served as a guest lecturer.

Church service called again, this time to build McCreesh Place, ninety units of single-room occupancy housing for formerly homeless men. The plan called for on-site social workers to provide support. I was in charge of the financing and developed the budgets, negotiated with the city for a soft second mortgage, arranged and closed the construction loan, and obtained a grant from the federal Department of Housing and Urban Development. It took us three years from start to finish.

Some of these organizational engagements lasted decades, like Urban Land Institute, University of North

Carolina at Charlotte (UNCC) advisory boards, and the Chamber of Commerce. Others ended, and new ones began. In 2004, I became a board member of Montreat Conference Center, the Presbyterian Church's largest national conference location. I would go on to chair that board for four years and serve as interim president for most of 2008. Meanwhile, starting in 2006, Melanie and I began a four-year term on the parents' council at the University of North Carolina at Chapel Hill (UNC-CH).

I left my company at the end of my fifteenth year, and my retirement event became a fundraiser for local housing ministries. It was dubbed "Sheltering Charlotte," and attracted business colleagues from around town and across the nation. We raised almost $40,000, all of which was given away through the new charitable fund Melanie and I had created.

Frank at the Sheltering Charlotte fundraiser

With time available, I moved deeper into service at the Presbyterian Church. I was invited onto the national strategy board of NEXT Church, a renewal movement in the Presbyterian Church (USA), and I also began serving on the board of directors for the Board of Pensions.

One day, while I was translating a Hebrew passage in my home office, the phone rang. It was a recruiter for

Habitat Charlotte. They wanted a new president. I protested that I was a seminary student, and she said the
board already knew that and they were sure I could do
both. Before I hung up, I knew I would take the job.

This litany of engagement could sound overwhelming,
but it took place over twenty-eight years in the same community, and had several important intersections. The church
is one; affordable housing another. A third nexus is education, at both my own alma mater, UNC-CH, and at institutions like the public school system and local universities.

Professional and business organizations are another.
Everyone should make participation in such organizations a normal part of professional life. Each organization
fulfills an important mission, but continuous community
and professional engagement has other rewards.

All of these endeavors created networking opportunities. Before we left Charlotte, my son would say that
I knew everyone in town. That is certainly not true in
a metro region of 2.4 million people, but I will say that
during my years in Charlotte there were very few of
the top business, political, and community leaders with
whom I did not have a personal relationship.

My approach was to weave all of these pursuits into
a single whole. I saw attending a Chamber of Commerce
reception, or a real estate program board meeting, or
the City of Charlotte Capital Advisory Committee, as
all part of my job. That job was to build the relationships
that would bring the company leads, deals, loans, capital,
employees, advisors, and ultimately success and growth.
When the CEO of one of our biggest clients asked me to
co-chair the Heart Ball that his hospital was sponsoring,
I readily accepted.

Frank in Washington D.C.

Engagement beyond my immediate job responsibilities has continued in my role as president of the Board of Pensions. I serve on two ecumenical boards. The Church Benefits Association is a group of fifty-five denominations, Catholic orders, and Jewish traditions that work together, bringing best practices and buying coalitions to the world of faith communities.

The Church Alliance is the lobbying arm of church benefit boards that works on legislative, regulatory, and judicial matters affecting the provision of benefits to workers in faith communities. It was the Church Alliance that successfully lobbied for the inclusion of congregations in the Paycheck Protection Program during the COVID crisis. That one action brought hundreds of millions of dollars to faith communities throughout the country.

By making community engagement an integral part of my career focus, we were always able to keep family at the center of our private lives. I spent three years with each child in Y Guides. Our daughter became a top swimmer in USA Swimming regional-level meets, and our son played basketball for his school in winter and top-level Amateur Athletic Union (AAU) teams in summer. We rarely missed a meet or a game. Melanie and I were usually at church on Sunday mornings, and played several seasons of mixed doubles tennis on Sunday afternoons.

One of the benefits of moving into leadership roles is often being able to set the schedule. I worked many hours outside nine to five, meeting people for breakfast or attending an after-hours reception. Travel was often multiple days at a time. I felt no compunction adjusting my schedule to be where I was needed for my family. I often planned my return home from traveling to coincide with the children's activities.

Rule your schedule so that it doesn't rule you. No one has ever accused me of not getting the job done.

CHAPTER 4

SEEKING EQUITY OWNERSHIP

According to Melissa Houston, writing in *Forbes* in August of 2024,

> *The dream of making a million dollars is more achievable than ever, provided you are willing to work for it. While there are various paths to financial success, starting (or owning) a business stands out as one of the most promising. Whether you're driven by the desire for financial freedom, the thrill of innovation, or the aspiration to leave a lasting legacy, entrepreneurship offers a viable route to significant wealth.*
>
> *Owning your own business can be a game-changer for your finances. Unlike a regular job where your paycheck is set, running a business means your earnings potential is limitless.*

Whether you start a business or take an equity stake in an existing business as I did, equity ownership is the key to creating wealth and, ultimately, financial freedom. A recent Fidelity study finds that 88% of millionaires did not inherit their wealth, but accumulated it over time. The most common means of that wealth accumulation is owning all or part of a business.

Recognizing opportunity

I was sweating in the summer heat as we stood at the door and rang the bell of a Georgian house in a gated community. What did this evening hold, and what would these people we had never met be like? My friend from real estate class who wanted me to be his boss had arranged a dinner at the home of Jim Cogdell, the sole owner of the Cogdell Group and Pahl's current boss.

Jim was charismatic, with a quick smile and flowing gray hair. Twenty years my senior, he had been seeking a junior partner for several years. Jim and his wife invited us in. The three couples sat down to a dinner of wonderful food and fine wine. Jim and I hit it off immediately, and I could tell we thought about business in the same intuitive way. After dinner, we all sat out back and talked well past midnight. The next week, Jim asked me to join his company.

I said no, because the goal of securing grant funding for CSN was still unfinished. Though unintentional, it was like waving a red flag in front of a bull. My loyalty and integrity were what Jim wanted in a partner, even more than my business-school polish and wide community network.

When I unexpectedly secured the grant funding six months early, I agreed to have lunch with Jim again. This time I was prepared. As we ate, Jim demanded an answer.

Me: "I'm very interested in what you are doing, but I can only consider it if I have an equity stake that comes from my efforts to grow the company. I don't have capital to contribute."

Jim: "Okay, how about fifteen percent of anything we do from here on?"

Me: "Fifteen percent in future projects is fine, but I also need fifteen percent of the operating company, if this is going to be a true partnership."

Jim: "What? It's been my company for twenty years."

Me: "I recognize that. Here's my proposal. We will have the company valued today. I will vest the fifteen percent on my fifth anniversary. You can fire me any time before that date by paying a sum equal to three percent of the current value for each full year I have worked. The fifteen percent in the properties we develop is not subject to vesting, and I will retain those interests. So, if it works, great. If not, you still own 100 percent of your company. Do we have a deal?"

Jim: "Yes, we have a deal. The one thing I worry about is whether you can sell."

Me: "I just sold you, didn't I?"

The operating company was valued at $10 million, and we began our partnership. Jim had shared his prospect list, and I knew two things: the business was about to take off, and the company didn't have the capacity to execute it.

Running the show

I arrived for my first day, January 2, 1996, with a business-school plan for orientation. I would run property management and finance, and Jim would continue with development while I learned the healthcare real estate business.

He had other things in mind. "I've been doing this a long time. I don't think you fully understand," he said. "You report to me. Everyone else reports to you." And then he left for the next thirty days to go fishing in Russia, leaving me to establish myself with the team of forty employees.

Our partnership was truly a blending of complementary skills. Jim was better at working a room and maintaining relationships than anyone I have ever known. By the time I joined the company, he already had hundreds of physician partners who had invested in the buildings in which they rented offices. There were hospital administrators whose lives Jim filled with fun and joy. We met in person annually with every limited partnership group at events that often turned into cocktail parties and dinners.

But Jim was limited. He developed each building himself. He couldn't scale the enterprise. I joked that when I arrived, the organization chart featured Jim in the middle with everyone else reporting directly to him.

Bookkeeping was done by balancing checkbooks, and each project's finances were in standalone spreadsheets. Consequently, Jim had managed to average one building a year at $8–$10 million of total development volume. Once, when he had landed a big job in New Orleans, he bought a condo in the French Quarter and moved there for two years.

My skills were different. Finance was easy for me. We consolidated accounting into a general ledger program. I developed proprietary legal structures that gave our non-profit hospital clients unprecedented access to capital. We developed management controls and hired staff. Our first year was devoted to finishing what Jim had already started.

In our second year, we developed $97 million in total volume, tenfold the running average of the prior twenty years. Jim's approach had always been to keep only five or ten percent of the equity for himself, with the rest going to the physician investors. Our equity piece that year was about $8 million, and my fifteen percent was worth $1.2 million.

At age thirty-seven, I had made my first million in business, and Jim had the biggest year of his career so far. We decided we should share the ownership with the team. He insisted I keep fifteen percent. He kept fifty percent, and we set aside thirty-five percent for the team in all future deals. The operating company was not included, and my vesting schedule rolled forward.

We began to professionalize the enterprise, hiring a new CFO and buying a general ledger package. All accounting was centralized. I promoted people to new roles and hired an increasing number of new professionals.

Our head of development, the friend who had recruited me to be his boss, complained bitterly to me that he was not earning as much as many of his graduate-school classmates. He suggested we develop a strategy to push Jim out. I explained that we were trading on Jim's relationships. I asked him how many of the current customers would leave Jim and follow him. His answer of "zero" ended the conversation. Shortly thereafter, he got his first six-figure bonus and resigned the following week.

The third year, I saw an opportunity for us to own 100 percent of a major new project. A hospital client wanted a retail setting, but no ownership. They became our anchor tenant in what was essentially a strip-mall development at one of the hottest intersections in the state. There were no doctor investors, and I engineered 100 percent loan financing.

With no money down, we now controlled the whole deal. We separated an out parcel, which was valued at $1.25 million and which was not included as collateral. Our total equity value once lease-up was completed would be almost $3 million. We paid Bank of America (B of A) the fee to secure our loan at a spread above LIBOR the second week of August 1998.

Two weeks later, the Russian ruble crisis hit and Russia defaulted on its foreign debt. In the worldwide financial flight to safety, interest rates plunged by over 1.5 percent. Our loan would have carried an interest rate of approximately 7.25 percent the day we paid the fee. The rate in September was now 5.75 percent. I got a voicemail from a B of A employee, whom I did not know, saying they could no longer honor the commitment.

I immediately called our attorney to ask if we had a binding contract. I was met with a long silence on the other end of the phone and then, "I can't talk to you about this. We are conflicted out on B of A." In fact, almost every law firm in Charlotte is conflicted out, because B of A made it a practice to do business with as many as possible for this very reason.

In contrast to my normally calm business demeanor, I threw the phone across my office, sending it crashing into the wall and ripping the cord out. I had no legal recourse, and was up against the largest bank in the country. I had put us in this deal, and we had no hope of closing it if we didn't get this loan. I found another phone and called the bank's head of North Carolina real estate. I said,

"Tell your boss I will be in his office in thirty minutes."

"Do you want me to be there?" he asked.

"Your call," I said, and hung up.

I was sick to my stomach and scared to death as I drove the thirty minutes to the B of A tower in the middle of the city. All I had was my relationship, but I knew Bill would see me. Just two weeks earlier, we'd had dinner together with Bank of America's soon-to-be vice chairman, Billy Payne, at the bank's golf outing in Pinehurst. Bill and I had several drinks together during the evening and professed our eternal friendship as we left the dining room arm in arm.

When I arrived, I was shown in to Bill's conference room. He had been up for forty-eight hours as B of A tried to unwind billions in loan commitments all over the country. He looked terrible. I sat next to him, keeping his capital markets guy and the head of NC real estate across the table from us. I wanted to emphasize our personal relationship. Sounding much more confident than I felt, I said,

"Bill, we have a solid contract and we've already paid the bank the fee to lock the deal. I expect the bank to meet its obligation."

He responded, "Frank, the bank simply can't lock a rate in the fives. What would you say to 6.35 percent?"

I stuck out my hand and we shook on the deal. Our project was not only saved, the profit had also just gone up by twenty-five percent. The capital markets guy piped up,

"So, do you want me to swap a rate right now?"

Relieved, and still angry that they had attempted to get out of the deal with a voicemail, I snapped,

"You go fund it however you want to. Your national head of real estate just promised me a fixed rate of 6.35 percent and I'm sure he intends to keep his word."

The loan closed at the new rate two months later. The capital markets guy was fired.

There were three critical elements in that brief encounter. First, the personal relationship I had built got me a hearing. Second, I expressed certainty of our position. Third, without blaming or threatening, it was clear that I expected the bank to do the right thing, and I gave them the chance to act.

From that day forward, I have never taken one of the anonymous conduit loans that get packaged into commercial mortgage-backed securities. I want to know the people lending me money, and I want them to know me. It certainly paid off in 1998, and it has been critical at other times since.

At the end of 1998, Jim named me president. At the end of 2000, I vested in the operating company and my name went up on the door.

One of our more innovative marketing ideas centered around the annual joint meeting of the North and South Carolina Hospital Associations. The conference was always held in Charlotte, the geographic and financial center of the combined states. We worked with our friends at NCNB/NationsBank/Bank of America to host the annual Cogdell Spencer wine dinner on the top floor of the bank tower, the tallest building between Washington and Atlanta.

Every year, we would have the bank's private chef combine with a local sommelier to create a seven-course wine dinner that was second to none. There was no budget, and it usually cost us $600 to $700 per CEO. But what company wouldn't pay $700 for four uninterrupted hours with its best customers?

To be invited, the hospital CEO had to be a client of ours. For the first couple of days at each annual conference, CEOs would ask each other, "Have you been invited?" All who attended agreed it was by far the best dining experience they had ever had. We were strict in not inviting anyone who was not working with us. When asked by a CEO if they might join (and we often were), we would invariably say, "Once we sign a contract to develop a building on your campus." Our business, and the attendance at the dinner, grew year over year.

In the late 1990s, eighty percent of all hospital spending went through non-profit hospitals. Our entire business was focused on those hospitals. I had developed a unique capital structure that allowed those non-profit entities to control the properties we developed on their campuses without them having to put up any money, nor having to consolidate liabilities onto their balance sheets.

Our buildings were on ground leases that reverted to the hospital in fifty years, and we gave an option to the hospital to buy the limited liability company we created for each building. However, for those fifty years, we had complete discretion to finance or even sell the assets. These structures were called synthetic partnerships.

One of our largest clients ran into real problems with Ernst & Young, their audit firm, who insisted that the sandwich of control required consolidation. The matter went all the way to E&Y's senior audit partner in New York. I flew up for the meeting. I managed to get him to admit that the documents gave us enough control to avoid consolidation, but he contended that the point was moot because no one would sign such a deal.

I said, "But here is the signed document."

He asked, "Why would any institution sign such a thing?"

"Because they trust us to act in their best interest," I explained.

He muttered something about no one trusting anyone when millions are on the line, unable to comprehend a business relationship built on trust. The assets were not consolidated in that audit, and our business grew again.

As the big accounting firms all encountered our ground-breaking structures, resistance began to grow. I can't say the Financial Accounting Standards Board changed the rules only because of our structures, but in 2003 sweeping changes came out concerning a new entity called the variable interest entity, which was aimed squarely at our structure and required consolidation.

Over the next few years, we explored potential mergers and partnerships that would have brought in additional private capital. We considered a deal with Starr-Sanders out of Birmingham, Alabama. All-pro quarterback Bart Starr was the frontman, and a true gentleman, but the money backing them was Richard Scrushy, CEO of HealthSouth.

Jim and I arrived at the brick-and-glass Scrushy Center in Birmingham. We were escorted by an armed guard to the top floor and led to a trophy room to await our audience. The room was oval-shaped, over twenty feet long. We began looking around, and Jim remarked, "He has every award money can buy." We both laughed. Scrushy's assistant appeared, and took us to the boss's private office.

We were greeted at the door by the HealthSouth CEO and ushered in. Scrushy apologized for the security and confided that threats on his life were frequent. The office was larger than most houses. To the left, about fifty feet away, was his private desk with two chairs. We were motioned to the right and crossed the thirty-by-thirty-foot carpet with the HealthSouth logo. We sat in the "living room," where we could see the nine closed-circuit screens and conference table the CEO used for remote meetings.

He told us that beyond the screens was his private area with a gym, showers, and a bedroom for when he just couldn't get away. He told us about his passions: his

Harley motorcycle, fronting a country rock band, and flying his own jet to the Gulf Coast on the weekends to vacation with his family. Jim was a pilot and we owned a plane, but we never went up without two pilots. It was simply reckless for a public CEO to put his company at risk by flying a jet alone. We barely got in a word edgewise concerning the potential merger.

Our one meeting in Scrushy's office brought an end to those discussions. Our final meeting with the Starr-Sanders executives was later that afternoon. We left Birmingham feeling that we had dodged a bullet. Scrushy would be convicted of financial fraud a couple of years later. Other discussions failed to find the right capital source for our business.

Moving into the big time

We continued to expand, and our investor base grew. By 2004, we had over 800 physician limited partners organized in 615 voting units, and we were also facing a crisis.

We were in a competition for a campus redevelopment sponsored by our largest client. We were the most experienced healthcare real estate firm in the southeast, but raising money for each project is hard work and takes time. We lost that competition to a new competitor who had limited experience, but did have the capital in hand and could write the check to the hospital without any waste of time. New entrants into our industry were raising lots of capital, and the competitive landscape had shifted.

It was time for a change.

After several private capital discussions fell through, we were approached with the idea of going public in late 2004. We interviewed law firms and investment banks. We selected Clifford Chance as issuer's counsel, and the investment banking teams of B of A and Citi as our bookrunners.

At the kickoff meeting on February 8, 2005, the collected experts threw up their hands and essentially pulled out when we revealed that none of our limited partnerships had mandatory roll-up provisions, and many required a unanimous vote to sell or consolidate. They told us to come back if we ever got the votes, never expecting to see us again.

I built the conversion model, aligning the ownership value of every building and partnership as a piece of the whole. Jim and I set out on the road. The relationships were everything. We led with the fact that neither of us was taking out a dime, and we ended up getting 612 affirmative votes out of 615 in a span of only seventy-five days. Two of the three who voted against were all in one tiny building with four partners, and so we just let them keep it. All the other partnerships voted to move forward with the real estate investment trust (REIT) and the associated operating partnership.

Four of the synthetic partnerships we had created for off-balance-sheet capital structures had no physician partners and did not produce cash flow that a REIT could count in its earnings. We donated these to the Foundation for the Carolinas and arranged for the hospitals to exercise their purchase options, thus creating the Cogdell Spencer Charitable Fund.

Going public is arduous under any circumstances, but this was a real bear. We had never done consolidated financial statements, and we had to create SEC-compliant financials. We hired a chief accounting officer to support our CFO. Converting thirty years of operating statements for approximately fifty buildings in thirty-eight partnerships took months and cost us over $1 million, which we drew down on our line of credit.

Jim felt that I had the financial skills and temperament to deal with the Wall Street analysts and investors. We decided that I would be the CEO going forward, and that he would be the non-executive chairman of the board. We set our salaries and contract terms exactly the same, except the share ownership, of which he still held the significant majority. I did all the negotiations with the investment banks, their underwriters, and stock analysts as the details of the IPO began to solidify.

The last week of August, Hurricane Katrina devastated New Orleans. Only three of twenty-four hospitals remained open, including the one we served with two large buildings. We had positioned a recovery crew on the Alabama border with roofing materials, carpeting, and drywall to make immediate repairs. The National Guard made our larger building its regional headquarters, and we provided sleeping and living arrangements for all the doctors on the hospital staff.

But the bankers wanted us to exclude these assets from the company, just six weeks away from the IPO. I argued that no tenants had missed rent, and it would be a betrayal to take those partners out of our deal because they were hit with a natural disaster. But the lead Citi analyst, Jonathan Litt, was insistent and did not want to give in.

Negotiating from my kitchen table one night at about 11:30 p.m., I pledged that the salaries Jim and I would be paid per our contracts would be put at risk and be used to make up any shortfall in cash flow from those two projects for thirty-six months following the IPO. Litt couldn't believe the offer, but he accepted it and we went forward.

For the second time, trust in our relationships had trumped the disbelief of New York–based financial types. We never had that guarantee called because the projects never saw any decline in cash flow. The physicians were loyal to us because we had been loyal to them during the storm and the aftermath.

After operations began to return to normal in New Orleans, we were called to the hospital CEO's office along with the owner of a competing building on campus. He said to our competitors, "You guys cut and ran when the hurricane hit and didn't return for over a month. These guys were here the next day and never closed. You will sell them your building, and I expect the deal closed by the end of the quarter."

Less than a year after the storm, we had gone public, wrote our competitors a check, and increased our campus portfolio at East Jefferson Hospital to 250,000 square feet. The power of loyalty, integrity, and being physically present is impossible to overstate.

The final two weeks of an IPO process are exhausting and nerve-racking. During the ten business days leading up to the IPO, we flew in a private jet all over the country, did eighty sales presentations, and ended up back in New York for pricing and the beginning of trading on the NYSE. Make no mistake, although the investment bankers pretend they are helping you, *you* are actually the product they are selling. Everyone is betting on the outcome—if the orders for your stock come up short, no one gets paid.

At our final sales call at the Teachers Insurance and Annuity Association of America (TIAA), we discovered that the head of their REIT investing unit was a classmate of mine from business school. Although we had not known each other at the time, the connection began another significant business relationship for me. Years later, I would be one of the first investors in the company he founded.

As Jim and I were riding to the pricing meeting at Citi's office in the financial district of New York, we began to assess our situation.

Jim: "Are we going to make the book and get out?"

Me: "We are or we aren't going home. We have our $4 million line of credit fully drawn and not enough cash flow to pay it back. We've got 800 partners who think we will start trading tomorrow. We will have to find a price that completes the book."

We had projected a price of $18 to $20 per share. I was on the phone with Fidelity's attorneys who wanted me to grant an exception for them to buy fifteen percent of the stock that was offered. Their traders were on the phone with the bankers offering $16 per share, confident that, without them, the offering would fail. The bankers insisted the price would be $17. When TIAA, our very last sales call, put in an order for ten percent of the stock, the book was made at $17 per share, and Fidelity was locked out.

After pricing, the bankers, lawyers, employees, and our families all went out for a celebratory dinner at the Tribeca Grill. Cocktails and champagne flowed, and everyone was indulging. The next morning, we were due at the New York Stock Exchange for breakfast at 8 a.m. with Catherine Kinney, the president of the NYSE. Leaving our hotel at 7 a.m., not everyone was ready to go, most notably Jim. We left anyway, calling a car to bring Jim later.

As CEO, I accepted the greeting at breakfast. I was given a replica of the famous bronze bull-and-bear statue by Isidore Jules Bonheur. We were all given special name tags, and led down to the trading floor. We stationed one of the junior bankers outside with Jim's credentials. Trading was scheduled to open at 9:30 a.m. With a scant five minutes to spare, Jim was ushered in and joined us on the floor. The famous bell rang.

We began trading as a publicly held REIT with a market value of $365 million and a dividend of $1.45 a share. Jim and I each bought 100 shares as the first trade. The operating company had been contributed at a value of $20 million. My fifteen percent of the company and my share of the properties brought me 595,000 shares, about $10 million in value. I had just turned forty-five. We made sure all employees got stock, seven of whom got more than $1 million from their project ownership.

At the New York Stock Exchange

Other things change overnight when you go public. Twelve hours earlier, we owed $4 million we couldn't pay back. The next morning, that $4 million obligation was rolled into a $100 million unsecured line of credit available on my signature. Bank of America led the loan syndication. We could issue more shares for capital needs at any point. We never had to raise deal-level equity again.

Thirty days later, we returned to the NYSE with our board of directors and our senior officers. We were scheduled to ring the bell to open trading. We wanted to create a strong visual, and so all wore customized scrubs with stethoscopes around our necks. This focus exclusively on healthcare real estate created a brand image that we used for years in promoting our new capital strength.

Accessing the public equity markets is like adding jet fuel to a drag-racing car—it's really powerful, and hard to control. We started buying buildings and developing others from the ground up. We grew so fast it was

dizzying. We bought one of our smaller regional competitors, solidifying our hold on the southeastern market.

In January of 2008, barely two years public, we bought
a healthcare design/build company with a national footprint. They had four times as many employees as we
did, but our access to capital dwarfed the private company. We returned to the NYSE to ring the bell for a
second time, with the combined management teams and
expanded board. This time, we wore lab coats and a ver-
sion of Jim's signature bow tie. We rang the bell that closed
trading at 4 p.m.

The acquisition made our company fully integrated
from initial design through property management. A full
forty-eight percent of every building's total cost went
through our operating company. We even owned a steel
fabrication plant that built pre-engineered walls. By September, our market value was in excess of $1 billion and
we had become the largest healthcare design/build firm
in America, as ranked by *Modern Healthcare*. Our annual
revenue hit $330 million.

On September 10, 2008, we did a follow-on offering
of stock after the market closed. It was oversubscribed
in forty-five minutes at $21 per share, a discount of only
two percent from the closing price of the day. I was urged
to issue more in the face of that seemingly unlimited
demand. Concerned about managing earnings per share,
I declined.

That Sunday, September 14, 2008, Lehman Brothers
declared bankruptcy and the music stopped.

The US credit markets froze. I was in a hospital CFO's
office when he got a call informing him that, for the first
time in history, the bond package he was counting on had

failed to attract sufficient investors. In the next ninety days, over half of all hospital capital projects in the United States were canceled. Traditionally, we signed forty percent of our contracts in the fourth quarter, but we didn't sign a single contract between September 14, 2008 and January 23, 2009.

Before Lehman, we had everything the markets wanted: slightly higher leverage, risk assets in the form of development, a fully integrated operating platform, greater operating leverage than any other healthcare REIT, and growth. After Lehman, the market wanted fortress balance sheets, low leverage, low risk, and cash flow rather than growth. Our stock price fell to half by year's end.

On the day we went public, I had told Jim that the company was necessarily for sale every day. Consequently, I made it my business to make friends with all the other healthcare REIT CEOs, whose companies were all bigger than ours. By the end of December, I had negotiated a sale of the company in a stock-for-stock swap that would have preserved our dividend and yielded our investors an exit approximately equal to our original value. Jim agreed, and we took the proposed transaction to the board for approval.

Our board rejected the offer.

One board member was a former bank president who, it seemed, was just playing with Monopoly money and wanted to see how things panned out. Another needed the $100,000 we paid directors annually and didn't want the gig to end. The two who had come with the recent acquisition were scared, fearing there would be recriminations if the company sold only one year after the merger. They convinced one other director, and the proposal lost five-to-four, over the objections of the chairman and the CEO.

Things got a lot worse. Our stock price continued to slide, leaving us unable to acquire anything because our cost of capital had more than doubled. We had to cut our dividend to preserve cash. On the worst day of my professional career, I faced our workforce and announced the layoffs of 128 people out of our 600 employees. We simply didn't have enough new business to keep them busy.

Our auditors didn't think we could renew our line of credit and wanted to give a qualified opinion, the kiss of death for a public company. I felt like the walls were closing in, and I could see them building the gallows in the courtyard.

I called all of the bankers who participated in our line of credit to a meeting at B of A. I had them seated in an open horseshoe in a large conference room. We passed around our financial statement and business plan. After walking them through our fiscal stability, I stood in the middle of the room and said,

> "I am going to ask each of you to commit for your institution. If anyone declines, the whole thing will fail."
> One by one, I approached each of the bankers, asking, "Will you renew your portion of our loan?"
> "Yes," responded all seven in turn.

Every banker had committed to the loan. I made them sign the commitment before they could leave the meeting. The company was saved, and Deloitte agreed to issue an unqualified opinion.

We issued more stock, and cut the dividend again. Fidelity finally bought in, and we began to build back. By August, the stock had doubled in price and we had seven regional offices around the country. I was named Real Estate Entrepreneur of the Year in the southeast by Ernst & Young, and was later inducted into their national Hall of Fame.

But the board now saw that even though we had the best operating company in the industry, our cost of capital was still too high when compared with the big players. We had been one-tenth the size of the largest competitor at IPO and had tripled in size, but that growth wasn't fast enough. The largest REIT had grown fivefold, and we were now one-fifteenth the market capitalization of the leader.

The board asked me to sell the company again.

We could see the snow coming down outside the windows, and the negotiators began to worry about getting home for Christmas. On December 23, 2009, in a New York conference room at a little past 5 p.m., we agreed to a stock-for-stock swap deal with Ventas REIT, including twelve years of tax protection on the assets of our operating partnership.

We would get shares, but not have taxes triggered for at least twelve years. The price per share was half of the deal one year earlier, as was the ongoing dividend. Ventas was the only option for us at the end, but they didn't know that and I had them bidding against a ghost. It was a good deal, and the only deal available to us.

But it was not to be. Jim went crazy at the board meeting, falsely accusing me of keeping two sets of books. His real problem was that he had learned Ventas was unwilling to continue his employment, but wanted me as part of their executive team. This had happened before with potential private partners, and, true to form, Jim tried to protect his role instead of his wealth. The vote was again five-to-four against, with Jim's four friends voting with him, and the acquired directors and my one nominee voting with me.

With two deals in the trash can, I told the board I could no longer be their CEO because they wanted to go in a different direction from the strategy I had twice laid out. I decided to take my non-compete payment and my pre-negotiated retirement package when my five-year contract ended on October 31, 2010. We made the announcement that I would step aside but continue as a member of the board. The continuity of planned succession was important to investors.

The board excluded Jim and me from the search process for my successor. The last thing Jim and I agreed on was that the person they chose to succeed me was incapable of leading our complex organization. With no development or design background, we feared he would drive the company into the ground.

We were right. I exited in October of 2010 and the new CEO came in. He would not go in my former office, and directed our head of asset management and the head of capital improvements to dispose of anything I had used by sending it to the dump. Still loyal to me, they called me and asked if I wanted my office furniture. My house was less than a mile from the office, and they showed up a few hours later at my garage with my walnut desk, matching credenza, lateral file, and leather chairs. (I am writing this account at that very desk.)

As I was leaving Cogdell Spencer, a publicly traded retail REIT offered me a job as their new CEO. It was nice to get the validation that outside observers thought I was doing a good job. They proposed a $2.5 million annual salary and significant stock ownership, but Melanie and I didn't want to get back on the treadmill. We had always lived well below our means, and the money wasn't really a factor. I turned them down, knowing there was a lot left in this world that I needed to pursue.

In January, the board called a secret meeting excluding Jim, the former CEO of the company we had acquired, and me. With a quorum of seven, including the new CEO, they fired Jim. A few days later, Jim called me and confessed that I had been right about everything: protecting him, working for his best interest, and even predicting that the board would dump him as soon as I was no longer there as CEO.

He asked which attorney I had used to negotiate my final exit package. He was considering suing the board to try and get his position and influence back. I said, "Jim, I can't have this conversation with you because I am still on the board, and even though I believe they were wrong to exclude us from their secret meeting, I owe my loyalty to the corporation." One week later, I resigned in protest. Both Cogdell and Spencer were gone. The company slid into the abyss.

Cogdell Spencer, Inc. was sold to Ventas for $768 million in cash with no tax protection, and at half the price per share I had negotiated with the same company. A cash transaction triggers deferred taxes and carries no ongoing dividends. I had taken my exit in cash a year earlier, trusting neither the new CEO's skill nor the board's judgment. My exit netted to about $10 per share, but Jim held on to the bitter end.

If we had taken the first deal, Jim would have had shares valued at approximately $48 million and a dividend of more than $3 million annually. Next, the deal with Ventas would have provided about $24 million in stock and a dividend for Jim of just under $2 million a year. The exit he ended up with—after being expelled from the board—was cash of $4.25 per share, or about $9 million. While I never had any hand in preparing Jim's tax returns, my suspicion is that most, if not all, of that $9 million may have been owed in taxes on earlier cash-flow distributions from the properties, taken over thirty-five years.

Despite passing on the better economic deals, both of us came out well. I had gotten tax-deferred annual dividends of $750,000 for four years, and Melanie and I had put most of that money away. My exit at about $6 million had some tax, but we were set. Jim had taken millions and millions out of the company, and owned a 1,500-acre equestrian and hunting spread, including his personal residence, valued at over $25 million, with no debt. He sold interests to his hunting buddies for about $10 million and today he lives in luxury, debt-free.

I opened a small investment company and began making equity investments, which have done well. Melanie and I created a donor-advised fund to support various charitable interests. And the bull market has restored our financial position to where we were at the peak of my public CEO days.

Not everything I tried after leaving Cogdell Spencer succeeded. I was the primary investor and director of a company that provided property management services for high-net-worth single-family homeowners. We hired a lead employee and managed to get a number of clients. We set up relationships with service providers. In the end, we just couldn't deliver the services at a price that was attractive to the customer and at a margin that would sustain the company. We shut things down, and I helped our key employee land a new position.

There are lots of lessons I learned coming through those years. Who you are aligned with is very important. Jim and I made some big mistakes in how we created our board of directors. We thought we had picked people who would support us, but we didn't thoroughly vet each member's motivations. Eventually, they pursued individual interests in opposition to us and the shareholders, and, unfortunately, we had already ceded authority.

After the merger in 2008, it became clear that the other CEO was ready to step back, but the COO of the acquired company had seen himself as successor and had aspirations to be CEO. With me at the helm, that was now impossible.

He began to undermine us at every turn, and I failed to fire him as soon as I saw the treachery. He survived my departure, but not the final sale to Ventas. That subsidiary was spun back out as a condition of the transaction, with the former COO now its CEO. He got what he wanted in being named CEO, but the company has been in steady decline, and is today one-sixth the size of the company we bought.

When you step into the public markets, you give up control in exchange for access to capital. The same is undoubtedly true when you take venture capital money. If you don't have personal or family capital, the trade-off you must eventually make in order to have an equity stake is using other people's money. When you decide to take that step, understanding the consequences is essential.

It's also easy to lose yourself in the fast-moving world of Wall Street. I remember a particular evening during the ten-day road show leading up to the IPO. We had an entourage of staff and investment bankers numbering about ten out for dinner in Chicago. I was handed the wine list. There was a $200 bottle of Brunello that I had always wanted to try. I ordered several for the table.

In that very moment, I knew I was breaching my ethics and normal boundaries. Two hundred dollars a bottle was a ridiculous amount to pay for wine. I rationalized that it didn't matter: the road show, the private planes, top hotels, limos, and dinners were all designed to get you, the product, in front of investors on time and on top of your game. It was costing $100,000, which would be paid out of the proceeds of the stock offering. So, what was a little wine with dinner?

Another time, I was invited to a golf outing at Pebble Beach in Monterey, California, with all expenses paid by the bank. I was the only CEO who flew commercial to get there. Our company had a plane for five years, but as a turbo-prop it was only used regionally in the southeast.

I caught a ride back to Charlotte on another CEO's jet. As a public CEO, you make a lot of money, and then you start getting lavish gifts. It becomes easy to believe that all this is normal, and of course you believe you deserve it because you work so hard. Ultimately, though, it's an illusion.

The way you structure any ownership deal can make or break you. I'm glad I went through the experience, and our family came out with financial rewards, but it was not without emotional scars. What I thought I understood intellectually was a very different experience emotionally when I went through it. For a public company, the pressure for growth in earnings per share is unrelenting. Being on-call 24/7 is not a normal way of living. It was hard to believe that tripling in size in just under three years was too slow.

Melanie would tell you the stress almost broke me. But then my faith saved me.

CHAPTER 5

BUILDING A
HAPPY LIFE

A happy life derives from creating wholeness within yourself and within your relationships. Yes, your professional skills and excellence in your career are part of the baseline for happiness. But while these are necessary, they are not sufficient by themselves. Whether you are still in school or already into a career, there are basic principles that you must put into practice to enhance your happiness. These include:

- the value of work,
- constant learning,
- willingness to lead,
- seeking adventure, and
- exploring beyond the normal.

And it's never too early to start.

Work

It was 5:30 p.m. on a Wednesday, an early spring day that was still cool in the late afternoon. I strained to hold my hand as high as I could in hopes of being selected. Each Wednesday, Taylor Blackwell, the publisher of the local weekly paper, would select the crew that would fold the papers for next day's delivery, as well as wrap and address those papers that went out through the mail to one-time residents who still wanted to keep up on the town news and gossip.

I was picked to work along with about a dozen other youngsters, boys and girls. The pay was $2.25 an hour. As the youngest at age ten, and, more importantly, the smallest member of the crew, my job was to sit under the folding machine as the newsprint whipped back and forth above my head. I had to complete the final fold as the paper dropped on me from above. Once a stack of ten accumulated, I pushed the whole stack out from under the folding machine far enough that another member of the crew could grab them. Had I stood up during my four-hour shift, I would have been decapitated.

As I grew, I kept getting picked for Wednesday evening, eventually working my way up to the mail center, rolling and labeling the papers that went all over the country. The only way I could reach the high table was to stand on an upside-down milk crate, but it sure was better than sitting under the loud and dirty folding machine. We got one break in each shift, and the orange Nehi soda only cost a nickel. There was no withholding, everyone was paid in cash, and clearing $8.95 a night felt like a fortune to a twelve-year-old in 1972.

I am sure my parents had no idea what I was doing, and would have been aghast at the dangerous work, but I learned a lot about work and pay, and even more about independence. I saved my earnings until I had enough to buy the genuine, all-leather baseball glove that hung in the window of the Western Auto hardware store. Endorsed by San Francisco Giants Hall of Famer Willie McCovey, that glove helped land me on the all-star team of our little league.

I would take other odd jobs over the next few years, and I landed a plum combination at the start of my junior year in high school. Our school used student bus drivers, and I signed up. At our initial training, the first question we were asked was, "Can you drive a stick shift?" Well, I had never even tried a manual transmission, and had gotten my driver's license in my parents' automatic.

So, I learned to drive a stick shift on an International Harvester bus. I didn't get a regular route, but that turned out to my advantage. I was involved in clubs and sports and so often drove the late bus, the longest after-school route, or I was a substitute for the north end of the county, which had the longest mileage route in the school. I ended up with dozens of hours each month, all at $5.35 an hour.

When I have told this story, many people can't believe that all our drivers were students. I ask them, "Would you rather have honor students and athletes driving, or the adults who now drive most buses for minimum wage on a part-time basis?" We were all afraid of Mr. Gadsden, who ran the transportation system, and we really toed the line. For the record, our high school drivers won the award every year for fewest accidents per mile driven, beating all the adult squads. Mr. Gadsden became one of five area superintendents.

At the same time, driving the family car gave me a chance to pursue other work. My brother was a sportswriter for the local paper, and I became the Friday night clerk, putting in the football scores as coaches called in from throughout the region. That was another regular paycheck that allowed me increasing independence. Two summers later, that relationship afforded me the chance to move from the scores desk to a sportswriter role, covering local events and profiling hometown athletes.

The summer after junior year in high school, the adventure and independence increased. I traveled alone to Gstaad, Switzerland. The route led from Charlotte to JFK Airport, to Frankfurt, then by train to Basel, Bern, and finally Gstaad, where I spent the summer living in a family-run hotel and restaurant. Basically, I was paid with room and board and got to keep tips as I ferried guests' luggage to and from their rooms. My duties included working as one of three maids each day as we turned the thirty rooms, and often as utility person in the kitchen in the evenings. But I was free to explore and live independently.

I befriended a young man from Saudi Arabia who spoke English and was desperate for company. He was staying at the posh Palace Hotel for the summer. I often met him at the hotel disco, where drinks and snacks were always on his tab and where we would dance with the younger set who happened to be staying in the hotel on any given night.

I entered the local tennis tournament and won the amateur division. My parents visited for a few days, tacking it on to one of my father's trips as part of the Fulbright Program. But mostly I was on my own.

It is never too early to understand the benefits, and limitations, of working for pay. Your own money feels different than an allowance, even if you do chores around the house as part of the arrangement. The independence and confidence I developed translated into other aspects of my life as I became accustomed to making decisions and living with the benefits or consequences.

For parents who have teenagers, there is another aspect to starting early that I did not have, but we have ensured that our children have—savings in a retirement account. As our two children earned money as high schoolers, mostly during the summer, we made them the following promise: if they would put 100 percent of their earnings in an IRA, we would replace it for them dollar for dollar. Both our kids thus started saving early and, by their mid- to late thirties, had substantial six-figure accounts. More importantly, both max out their contributions where they work, a commitment they learned early.

Learning

I sat in the teachers' lounge with two other students waiting for Mr. Graybill to arrive. Leslie, Nancy, and I were ready to dive into geometry. We were the only ninth graders taking the subject. Everyone else, even the advanced kids, were just starting algebra. A year before, my older sister had said that "eighth-grade math" was a waste and my parents should insist that I join the ninth graders taking algebra.

When Leslie and Nancy heard about my jump, their parents insisted they do the same. So now, we were a class of three with the head of the math department teaching us during his planning hour. The class behind us had twenty-five kids who skipped into algebra, and Mr. Graybill knew he would have a full room the next year.

Leslie and I would end up as co-salutatorians at our high school graduation. All three of us joined the eleventh graders in Algebra II Trig the next year as we started high school. Leslie and Nancy ended math in what was then called analysis, and pursued other interests during their senior years. I stayed with math, and Mr. Shaver taught me calculus one-on-one in my senior year.

Just like three years earlier, those twenty-five who followed our lead created a full calculus class for Mr. Shaver the year after I graduated. As for me, I placed out of calculus in college, one of the many things that gave me great curricular freedom to explore other courses. I learned French in high school, and likewise placed out of the first few levels at UNC.

I not only learned another language, I learned to play music. My brother is a talented musician who has co-written and recorded three albums. I was not so gifted. I learned to play trumpet by force of will and constant practice. I have good rhythm, but a tin ear. I can't carry a tune singing, and I can't play by ear. But by God, I learned to read music and learned to play. I was always assigned the first trumpet part, but never first chair. Two sisters, both of whom were better musicians than I, always sat to my left.

Our high school band director was a very creative guy. Instead of selling band candy or Christmas wrapping to fund the marching band uniforms, he created a performance band, the Blue Notes. We met at a special period during the day, the twenty-four best musicians in the school. We recreated the big band sound of the

1940s and '50s. We played for weddings and corporate events at $300 a show—cheap for a big band, and great for funding the program.

I could never ad lib my solos. I knew which songs they came in, and so I would practice them over and over at home. When the time came for my solo, I would stand and look for all the world like I was jamming, but every note was well rehearsed.

While excellence in school is critical to your future options, it is far from the only learning that is available. At nine or ten years old, I joined the Children's Drama Workshop. CDW was run by a wonderful teacher, Connie Welch, who had been on stage professionally in New York before moving to our small town with her husband, a music professor.

My first lead role was Edmund in *The Lion, the Witch and the Wardrobe*, when I was eleven years old. I had other leads playing characters like Tom Sawyer and, later, Henry Drummond in *Inherit the Wind*. Growing up on the Davidson College campus, I even took a mime class with the legendary Marcel Marceau when he came to perform.

All that time on stage would prove invaluable in my future endeavors. I have always been comfortable in front of an audience, and at this point in my career have delivered more speeches than I can count. Whether sales, or in front of city council, or delivering a sermon, or answering questions before 2,000 onlookers at our denominational general assembly, the ability to engage an audience is a skill that everyone needs for leadership.

Academics, music, and theater were all critical in my development. None, however, gave me the high that athletic mastery did. I started taking tennis lessons at age nine. By twelve, I was playing in tournaments sanctioned by the United States Tennis Association (USTA), but with limited success.

By high school I had gotten a lot better, and my doubles partner and I went 24-2 over two years, winning the conference championship and making it to the state tournament. We lost in the quarter finals. While I enjoyed our success in doubles, I desperately wanted to play number-one singles. My partner was a year older, and I could never beat him to take over the top spot.

As a rising senior, and with my partner now off to college, I knew it was my time to be number one. To my chagrin, a hot-hitting sophomore showed up and consistently beat me again. Number two was the best I could do. But we teamed in doubles and did fairly well. By the time I was eighteen, I was ranked twenty-fifth in North Carolina in singles and fifteenth in doubles. I knew I would never be among the elite players at the college level, but tennis has been important for my relationships and enjoyment my entire life.

Basketball was another story. I was playing junior high ball and was a gym rat watching the Davidson College team at many practices. At about age thirteen, one of the coaches asked if I wanted to work with him for a half hour after practice finished each day. I jumped at the chance. He taught me how to shoot a jump shot from above my head instead of a set shot from my chest. I became a starter on the junior high team.

That coach, who was only twenty-three at the time, was Jim Larrinaga, who became head coach at the University of Miami. Coach Larrinaga didn't have to help a kid after practice, but he cared about people and helped me gain mastery of a skill.

In 2006, Larranaga led his eleventh-seeded George Mason squad to the National Collegiate Athletic Association (NCAA) final four. I emailed him "Congratulations" the week before their appearance in the national semi-final game. Instead of a quick "Thanks" or no response at all, as I expected, I got a lengthy personal email that recalled our time together. That is personally engaged leadership.

But I gave up basketball in tenth grade, thinking I should concentrate on tennis. While I certainly improved my tennis game, I missed playing ball. So, I found another outlet. I was part of the first class in North Carolina to go through school in fully racially integrated classes, but that didn't mean we mixed when choices were available.

As I arrived in high school, I found out that all the Black kids went to the gym during lunch while the white kids gathered in the cafeteria. While lunch was consumed, the real action in the gym was pick-up basketball. So, I went to join in. The first day, I got there after the teams had been chosen. The winners stayed up, and challengers would then come on. No one picked me for their challenge team.

The second day I got there on time, only to discover that the "rules" required that the two captains were determined by who hit the first two free throws. I was too far back in the line to even get an attempt. Neither captain chose me, and again I sat out the entire time.

I resolved to get to the front of the line. The next day I ran to the gym and made it in time to be third in line. The first guy made the shot. The second guy missed. Here was my chance to be captain and pick a team. The shot went up, bounced on the back of the rim, up above the hoop, off the front rim and out. I had missed, and no one picked me for their team.

For the next week, if I ran to the gym and made the shot, I became a captain. This little society would not violate their own rules. I had stayed every time I had been excluded and watched every game. I knew who the better players were. Now that I was a captain, I picked a good team. We won, and winner stayed up.

The first time I was captain, my team went undefeated through the entire lunch period. I became an interesting oddity. I was good. Every time I bested my direct opponent, an audible gasp arose from the bleachers. Gasps turned to jeers as I blocked shots and twisted for layups. But the jeers were not directed at me, but at the poor soul who drew the short straw and faced me.

For several weeks, if I was not a captain, I didn't play. But as I demonstrated my value to whatever team I was on, things began to change. The jeers stopped. It was no longer an embarrassment for me to win a confrontation. I quit running to be a captain, because I was always picked to be on a team.

I was the only white person in that gym, but what I learned was not solely about race. It was about cultural norms, about performance, about acceptance through the combination of conformity and contribution. I had committed to the process, and been rewarded and accepted.

My senior year, I decided to go out for varsity basketball because a lot of the team had graduated, the football coach was assigned to take over, and I figured if we lost every game by twenty points I could get a lot of playing time. Boy, was I wrong. I made the team, but the new coach focused on conditioning, making us run suicides, a brutal drill involving up and back touching each succeeding line and changing direction.

We were a miserable group and started the season 4-4, with little offensive scheme and no creative solutions. Then, the conditioning kicked in. We literally ran past every team we played from then on. In one game against West Charlotte, I was in at the end of the first half. I took a pass on the fast break and laid it in for our fiftieth point as the buzzer rang. In two eight-minute quarters, scoring fifty points is almost unheard of. We won the game by thirty points.

I was one of only three white kids on the team. I didn't start, and so was the only white player who began each game on the bench. Our assistant coach, who was white, got mono and left the team. Our coach, also white, insisted that I sit next to him.

He would become so emotional, pounding the floor with his hands, that he could neither wear his wedding ring nor make executive decisions. I took over all substitutions, play-calling, and timeouts. We never lost again, winning our conference championship by beating two powerhouse teams on consecutive nights. I had not played a minute in thirteen straight games, and was sorely disappointed.

The assistant coach returned for the state playoffs, but I, now the lucky charm, had to sit beside the coaches. We played the eventual state 4-A runner-up and lost.

But with six minutes to go, down eight, the two coaches turned to me and asked, "So what should we do?" We were getting killed on the boards, and I suggested we start fouling to extend the game and limit their second-chance points. It didn't change the outcome.

My basketball experience, from pick-up at lunch, to varsity games, to not playing at all during the second half of the season, gave me a lot of insight into leadership, racism, and expectations about roles and responsibility. I feel fortunate that I learned so much as a very young person about how the world runs on unwritten rules and norms. Our coach evolved from that first season. Years later, he would lead a team to capture the state championship, and eventually he was inducted into the North Carolina High School Athletic Association Hall of Fame.

Three years later, basketball would allow me to penetrate another culture that was initially foreign to me. I played point guard for the University of Regensburg as an exchange student, bringing a novel brand of basketball to the German university league, which often played a very methodical style. My freewheeling approach frequently left opponents staring as I would grab a rebound and go end to end or dunk off a lob pass. At six foot one and weighing only 165 pounds, I could jump higher than I ever had before or since.

More importantly, I was building friendships and traveling with classmates I would never have known without the bonds of being teammates. Every practice and most gamedays ended at the local brewery, where we shared cold beer and conversation. I remember those relationships much more vividly than any on-court plays.

Leadership

At the last spring assembly of fifth grade, my best friend, Peter Raiford, and I sat beside each other in the auditorium of Davidson Elementary School. We were waiting to hear who would be next year's co-captains of the safety patrol. The co-captains, who were always sixth graders, organized which posts the safety patrol volunteers would cover. Each road crossing to the school grounds had to have one. The captains then went to the office and picked up the American flag, which was raised each morning and had to be taken down at the end of the day.

We had both applied. We also knew that in our racially integrated school, one captain had to be white, and the other had to be Black. We fit the bill. Our names were called, and we went up on stage. Mr. Roberts, our principal, presented us with the white sash-and-belt combination that bore the blue-colored captains' badges.

Two years later we were both in junior high, a combination of four elementary schools, so much bigger and complex to navigate. Peter and I were co-captains of the JV basketball team, and we both won seats on student council. By high school, Peter had turned to other interests, but I ran for student council and was elected every year from seventh to twelfth grade.

Although I made the council every year, I was never elected as the chair. Never the ultimate leader, I had to swallow my pride and remain committed to the work as a participant. I felt it was better to be in the decision-making group than outside it.

My junior year in high school, word came down that the school system wanted more input from its students. Each of the ten high schools was to send a representative to the newly formed Student Coordinating Council. I volunteered to represent our school, ran for vice chair, and was elected.

With quick success among the ten representatives on the SCC, I decided to attend the NC State Student Council Convention. There, I ran for vice chair of the statewide organization, using the Wiener King branding slogan of "Big Frank." I got dozens of their buttons and bumper stickers, and handed them out liberally. I was roundly defeated, and ended the convention with no ongoing role.

The next year it was easy to get elected as chair of the SCC. The school board decided that the chair of the Student Coordinating Council should sit with voice but no vote at each meeting. Thus, in 1977, I became the first student representative to the Charlotte-Mecklenburg school board. That role took me to all ten high schools to garner student input from around the county, allowing me to hone my speaking skills even further.

I will admit that, one time, I abused the power to come and go from high school, and even signed out other students in the office. My doubles partner and I had heard that Arthur Ashe was coming to town and would hit with tennis players on a court set up on a street in the city's center. I signed us out, and we were first in line. My partner went first. Then I stepped onto the court. I exchanged groundstrokes with Ashe, moving him around a little bit. He called a halt to groundstrokes, and everyone else in line only got volleys.

We were interviewed on the spot by local TV crews for the midday news programs. "What was it like to hit with a Wimbledon champion?" we were asked. "You guys look like real tennis players—where do you play?" We didn't realize that our teachers were watching on their lunch break. Because teachers were not allowed to leave campus during the school day, my penance was to bring back their favorite sandwiches for the next month whenever I signed myself out. Everyone was happy with the outcome of our adventure.

Never believing that I had too much to do, or couldn't manage it all, I put myself forward whenever the chance arose. I was a patrol leader in scouts, president of the French Club, and captain of multiple sports teams, among other things. It is never too early to learn leadership, and the more you practice it the more effective you become.

One leadership role often leads to another. Bruce Jenner (before he transitioned to Caitlyn) was on tour celebrating his victory in the Olympic decathlon. I was selected to be one of the student interviewers for the local PBS station. So, by the time I was seventeen, I had been a part of the school board deliberations, been on TV, put copy in the newspaper, appeared in multiple plays, played lead trumpet in a big band, and spoken before audiences all around the county. Most of that came as a result of showing up and putting myself forward.

The most important turn in my early life came as a result of building a diverse, but visible, resume of activities: sports, leadership, academics, service. I was nominated by our school for the Morehead Scholarship to the University of North Carolina (now the Morehead-Cain Scholarship). This is still the state's most prestigious scholarship, drawing competition from prep schools throughout the US and England.

By the time finals weekend in Chapel Hill rolled around, I had already won the Angier B. Duke Scholarship at Duke University and the Daniel Webster at Dartmouth College. Finals consisted of a series of interviews with three panels of alumni and other prominent state leaders. Many of the candidates went in terrified, and came out sure they had failed. Half would end up winning the scholarship.

I was so comfortable talking with adults and in front of an audience that my interviews were filled with laughter and meaningful interchange. I came out a winner. My bags had been packed for Dartmouth, where I had already worked out for the tennis coach, but the Morehead Scholarship changed my mind, and ultimately the trajectory of my life.

I was not good enough to play varsity tennis at UNC-Chapel Hill. The desire to run for campus-wide office likewise left me, and I never tried for that kind of recognition again. Instead, I joined Chi Psi fraternity, an extraordinary collection of men, the largest fraternity on campus, and the only fraternity that was racially integrated and welcomed openly gay brothers. In 1978, that was simply extraordinary.

I poured my efforts into intramurals at Chi Psi and into leadership of the fraternity. I held several roles, and in my junior year stood for election as president. I lost again. Instead, I was elected secretary of the executive council, a bitter consolation prize. But I never withdrew. As I had done in high school, I volunteered to represent

Frank with fraternity roommate Rodney Phillips

us on a larger scale, and was elected as the southeastern representative to the national council.

Through Chi Psi I built relationships with over 200 men, many of whom have been lifelong friends. It is also where I encountered industrialist Oliver Rowe, our national president. Oliver called us his "Supermen," and consistently preached excellence in all things. I can trace my commitment to that concept to my time at Chi Psi and the example my brothers set.

Our fraternity chapter at Carolina maintained a collective GPA of 3.4 on a 4.0 scale, and has produced more Rhodes Scholars than most colleges in America. Brothers have founded investment banks, started digital companies like Ancestry, won Emmys, led national non-profits, and become professors, attorneys, judges, physicians, authors, musicians, and, in one case, served as governor of North Carolina.

I recognize that I had many advantages that led to an all-expense-paid scholarship to a top university. Most people will not have that opportunity. But everyone can apply themselves in the classroom, put themselves forward for leadership, participate in things that improve the community, and find some element of physical activity or competitive pursuit.

All of these things, and particularly all of them in combination, create opportunities in your life. That should be your goal. Maximize your own talents for the pure pleasure of it, and you will discover that your next opportunities are derived from those same pursuits. More often than not, I was not number one in any particular area. However, even when disappointment hit, I stayed committed to the larger organization. That allowed me to develop leadership skills that would later help propel me to the top job time after time.

Adolescence

A final word on adolescence: seek older companions from whom you can learn. For me, these relationships came in many forms. At the newspaper, I sat and talked with men and women who were decades older than I and who had been in that business for years. Within my fraternity, I was first guided by older brothers and then became that same leader for others. Growing up in a small town with a college campus provided other opportunities.

When a schedule conflict with the Blue Notes caused me to drop out of the band program for good in eleventh grade, I took my music skills to the college pep band. The pep band was small, and needed all the help it could get. We played at every football and basketball game, and we also hung out and shared a beer before or after. I became friends with a number of the college students from whom I learned, and with whom I am still in touch today. Although I didn't attend Davidson, I currently serve on its Board of Visitors.

Jeff, another high school friend, was very into radio, and introduced me to the students who ran the local college station. I was able to be on air from time to time, and would later host a radio show during one summer when I was in college. Jeff went on to build a career in radio and music after he finished college.

Two of those friends became two of Melanie's and my closest friends. Both were in our wedding, along with Jeff. Even someone just a few years older often has perspectives that teenagers would be well advised to learn from. It also tends to thrust you ahead of your peer group in all aspects of life, as interacting with those older than you becomes less and less intimidating.

As you enter college and then begin working life, everyone in authority over you will be older than you. Developing confidence in dealing with your elders is a critical skill to early advancement and long-term success.

Adventure

"Climbing," I yelled up to the guy sixty feet above me. "On belay," he shouted back down, and I began my twelfth ascent of the morning. As the last climber in our group of five, I had the job of taking out the protection (odd-shaped chocks and bongs) from the cracks between rocks as I went. My hands stung as I worked the stubborn metal shapes out of each crevice and clipped them on my belt. It was 11 a.m., and we had been on the north face of Mount Arrowhead for five hours already. At 12,000 feet of elevation and with no sun, the temperature never got above freezing.

I could take the protection out because my top-rope belay partner had me tight and provided all the protection I needed. Unable to feel my fingers, thirty feet above the ledge from which I began, I felt myself peeling off the rock face. I calmly yelled, "Falling," as we had been taught on this five-week mountaineering course.

My perlon rope, a 7/16-inch-wide tether tied to my climbing belt, fed over a rock ledge, and my belay partner could neither see me nor feel me inching up the rock. The rope was slack and the belay was late. Although perlon is incredibly strong, it also stretches. I fell thirty feet, passing my starting point and continuing downward another ten feet.

I broke the cardinal rule of rock climbing and looked down. I was dangling 1,000 feet above the boulders below, and was now ten to twelve feet away from the rock face. I began shaking with fear. The only way to get back to climb again was to begin swinging my body until I had enough momentum to grab on to a handhold and scramble up to the beginning ledge. When I made it up to the top of the pitch, a storm was rolling in and our leader decided we should descend, giving up the assault on Mount Arrowhead.

That failed attempt was the penultimate event on our National Outdoor Leadership School course. A month earlier, we had started with eighty-pound packs and barely made it a mile before our arms and legs went numb.

We ate and slept as tent groups. I shared my space with Gerry, a twenty-year-old college student, and Julie, a twenty-eight-year-old schoolteacher. At seventeen, I was the youngest of the twenty who set out into the Wind River Range in Wyoming.

Our final event was a five-day overland trek with no food. By then, the packs were lighter because we had eaten the twenty pounds of food we each carried from the resupply ten days earlier. We were all much stronger, and could easily cover fifteen miles a day off-trail in our small groups. I am forever grateful I did this adventure, and would never do it again.

Adventure comes in many forms, not just physical peril and exhaustion.

We sat silently on the bus, passports in hand, nervous as the East German soldiers moved from row to row examining our documents. The tension was heightened by the fact that they all looked about our age as college sophomores, and each carried a Kalashnikov automatic rifle.

Once we were all cleared, we proceeded through Checkpoint Charlie for our bus tour of East Berlin. The primary stop was the Pergamon Museum, which held amazing

Middle Eastern artifacts including the Ishtar Gate of Babylon, which had been taken apart on site and reassembled in Germany.

On the way back toward the Berlin Wall, our East German guide pridefully pointed out all the wonderful elements of life in Berlin behind the Iron Curtain. She pointed to the Palace of Justice, where the people often gathered for cultural events and to frequent the excellent restaurant that had been opened there. She showed us another venue that had a modern discotheque, where she said that young people loved to meet and dance to the latest music. Back at Checkpoint Charlie, we went through an exit search to ensure that no East German citizens had stowed away on our bus heading to freedom.

The next night, our group of exchange students was slated to attend a performance of Bertolt Brecht's *The Threepenny Opera*. I had another plan. In 1980, the US dollar was exchanging with the Deutsche Mark at a rate of about two to one. West German banks would sell East German marks at four to one against the Deutsch Mark, but would give you nothing for East German marks themselves. So, for $25, I bought 200 East German marks and decided to go on my own to discover how folks lived on the other side of the Wall.

There were two problems: it was illegal to take East German currency into the country and, without a visa, you could only visit on the date you went through the checkpoint. I put my contraband currency in my underwear, presented my passport to the guard, exchanged the required ten Deutsche Marks (one to one for East German marks), and walked through Checkpoint Charlie into East Berlin.

It was already after 6 p.m., and I made a beeline to the Palace of Justice. Having attended a German university for the entire semester, my language skills were good enough that I could navigate easily. I asked the head waiter for a table, and was seated by myself at a table for two.

I placed my order, but before my food came another man was seated at my table—a common event in Europe and mandatory in East Germany, where everything, including seats, was limited. We talked hardly at all. I didn't know if this burly guy was just a hungry office worker, or a Stasi agent following me.

For dinner I had ordered the largest steak, plus potatoes, a salad, dessert, and wine. I figured I could afford it with my 200 marks plus ten now safely transferred to my wallet. I enjoyed the meal in silence. When the bill came, I was shocked: 9 marks 80. I felt an opportunity and a problem beginning to materialize: how could I possibly spend another 200 marks?

From the Palace of Justice, I headed for the building that housed the disco. It wasn't hard to spot, with a line out the front door not unlike Studio 54 in New York City, where I had been a year earlier. But the line moved slowly. Soon I figured out that those waiting were admitted only when an equal number of patrons left. The line crept forward in ones and twos. After forty-five minutes, I was on the threshold. Finally, the door opened and a young man exited. I was shown in by the doorman.

Inside, it looked like a lot of dance places in the West. Low lights, some flashing. Loud music and a crowded dance floor. I made my way to the bar and ordered a beer. "We don't serve beer," the bartender yelled back, "We have vodka." "Uhm, I'll take vodka and Coke." It came with a lemon as garnish. "Seventy finnig," he demanded. I was down to 199.50. As I stood watching the dancers, the song ended and the lights came up.

Like a giant game of musical chairs, everyone scurried for a seat—everyone but me. A bouncer approached and said, "Sit down or you will have to leave." I had waited almost an hour to get in, and I wasn't about to get kicked out. I scoured the room as the staff began to count people, making sure no one had gone in or out unauthorized.

They were good at what they did. There was only one empty chair, at a table for four, the three other places occupied by East German soldiers. I approached them and asked if the spot was free, and they invited me to join them.

The count confirmed, the lights went down and the music cranked back up. My tablemates asked where I was from. I made them guess. "Bulgaria. No, Czechoslovakia. Wait, Poland." My German was good, but they could tell I wasn't native. What they couldn't imagine was an American walking into their disco. They asked if I spoke Russian, and I asked if they spoke English. Both questions were answered with "No," which led to an evening spoken entirely in German.

I became instantly popular, buying drinks for everyone who came to our table. My new friends in the East German Army procured dance partners for me. Aside from the lights coming up every hour for the musical-chairs head count, it was a lot of fun. It seemed everyone there wanted to talk with me. I was translating the English lyrics that were blaring. People were most amused by my rendering of "Highway to Hell" by AC/DC.

My three uniformed compatriots and I were all aged between eighteen and twenty, and each of them knew exactly how many days they had left to serve. We talked about our lives and global politics. They bemoaned the fact that they couldn't go to Paris to see the Louvre, and asked me to tell them about my recent trip there.

I told them their government was afraid they wouldn't come back. They protested that of course they would return; this was their home. I said, "Look at the Wall. The guns are pointed in at you guys, not at us in the West. No one is trying to sneak their way to this side of the Wall" (my own adventure notwithstanding).

They asked why the US was boycotting the 1980 Olympics that were being hosted in Moscow. I explained that it was in response to the Soviet invasion of Afghanistan. They said that made no sense, because sport and suppression of terrorists were not related. I had to agree. However, later that year, I would take a train across Germany to the Rhein-Main Air Base to register for the draft, as President Carter required in his executive order.

Everyone was a little drunk and having a grand old time. I looked at my watch for the first time in hours. I was shocked into reality and sprang from the table. It was 11:45 p.m., and I had to be out of East Berlin before the calendar turned to the next day. I put the rest of my money on the table, thanked them for a wonderful evening, and bolted for the door. As I sprinted toward Checkpoint Charlie, I knew the stakes. Arrive late with no visa and you couldn't leave, nor could you stay. The only remaining alternative was a holding cell and Stasi interrogation.

I rounded the corner and saw my goal, the brightly illuminated sign in German stating, "You are now leaving the Soviet zone." I sprinted all the way, presenting my receipt for the ten marks I had earlier exchanged with the guard at exactly 11:58 p.m. He asked, "Didn't you buy anything?" I replied, "No, just walked around, and here's the ten marks." He released me into West Berlin.

Exploration

"Pop" went the bottle of wine as I pulled the cork. I poured two glasses and handed one to her. "It's a pretty spectacular view, the clay tile roofs, the lights, the Arc de Triomphe and the Eiffel Tower in the distance," she said. "It really is," I answered.

A year older than me, Mary had been my best friend since junior high. We had never had a romantic relationship, although I had kissed her once on the night I took her to her senior prom. "How long did it take you to get here?" she asked as we let the sound of the street below wash over us. "A day and a half hitchhiking," I replied. "I made it almost to Frankfurt the first day, and slept in Dad's World War II sleeping bag under a highway overpass. The rest of the way today." In the following three days, we went to the Louvre, the Musée d'Orsay, and out to Versailles.

Two years later, I would again find myself in Paris, sitting in a café on the Champs-Élysées. As I savored a glass of wine and wrote a few postcards, who should walk by but Jim Nabors of Gomer Pyle fame. I called out, "Hey, Jim," and he stopped. I invited him to sit and join me for a glass of chardonnay. He took me up on the offer, and we sat and talked for a half hour. I paid for the wine and we said goodbye. Had I just let a celebrity walk on by, I would have never learned about his family, and his perspectives on Andy Griffith and the Mayberry shows in which he had been featured.

Over the eight months I was in Germany studying, I took every opportunity to see the great sights of Europe. In addition to Paris, I took the train to Vienna, Venice, Munich, Rome, Florence, and Berlin. I came away with a first-rate education in art and history. I also picked up a slew of German language credits.

When I returned to Chapel Hill for my junior year, I declared German literature my major, and needed only four classes in four semesters to graduate. I also began a grand exploration. I asked everyone I knew to pinpoint their favorite class and professor.

Free from graduation requirements, I signed up wherever the best experiences were on offer. I took classes on the theory of education, the French Revolution, the philosophy of language, crime and punishment, art history, and social dance, along with honors in German, economics, accounting, and Spanish.

Here's what I tell young people: unless you already know you want to be an accountant, an engineer, or a doctor, your undergraduate major doesn't really matter. Pursue the liberal arts and humanities. Broaden yourself. Learn about the world. Everything you'll need to specialize in for your future career you will learn in graduate school.

For example, if you think you are interested in business or finance, business is the worst undergraduate major for you. If you go for an MBA—and you will have to, unless your family is going to give you lifetime employment— the first semester of every MBA program will cover everything you learned in undergraduate business.

As a CEO who has hired thousands of employees, I always look for liberal arts majors. It's easy to teach an English major finance, but hard to teach a finance major to think critically and write convincingly. I want an investment analyst who was a history major and has some understanding of world culture. Spreadsheets are easy, and first-year MBAs all learn the capital asset pricing model. If you want to be a lawyer, political science or sociology may prove most beneficial.

I took other chances to boldly explore. In my freshman year, I learned that an obscure band who had only one hit record was coming to Davidson College for a concert. My two good radio friends were juniors and would be interviewing the band after the show. I drove to Davidson and set it up that I would carry the audio equipment for them.

We saw an amazing concert with 400 students in Love Auditorium. Those three guys put out a wall of sound like nothing I had ever heard, with no dubbing or recorded support. The radio team headed backstage, with me as the tech guy.

For over an hour we sat and talked with the band members—Andy Summers, Stewart Copeland, and Gordon Sumner—about their music. Most of the conversation was between Andy and Stewart, who debated whether their music was something new or derivative of great rock and roll of the past. Gordon focused on eating his grapefruit and recovering from the intense physical performance he had given minutes before.

Gordon had adopted the stage name Sting, and The Police would go on to make mega-hits. Being bold, and having relationships that could bring me into private venues, led to a once-in-a-lifetime experience.

Well, *almost* once in a lifetime. In college, I was a big *Rocky Horror Picture Show* fan. Anyone familiar with the movie knows Tim Curry stars as the outrageous lead character, Dr. Frank-N-Furter. The movie was released in 1975, and was sweeping through campuses by 1978 when Curry signed with A&M Records as a solo artist.

His tour brought him to Durham, North Carolina in 1980. Using information I had gleaned from my radio and music industry friends, I showed up at the venue, projecting the persona of a major record label rep, promoting airtime on regional FM stations. I talked my way into the VIP box, took in the whole show, and met briefly with Curry afterward. Fortunately, Tim dropped his musical ambitions shortly thereafter and went on to have an extensive acting career, starring in the movies *Home Alone 2* and *Clue*, among others.

CHAPTER 6

EVOLVING WITH
A LIFE PARTNER

According to Warren Buffett:

> "You want to associate with people who are the kind of person you'd like to be. You'll move in that direction. And the most important person by far in that respect is your spouse. I can't overemphasize how important that is. Marry the right person. I'm serious about that. It will make more difference in your life."

Research shows definitively that those who are married and stay married to the same partner have many life advantages over those who never marry or those who divorce. Building a life with a spouse would find favor with the great Ben Franklin—it will make you healthy, wealthy, and wise. Additionally, it will make you happier over a lifetime. This has certainly been true for Melanie and me.

Binding yourselves together

We found each other early in our lives. We began dating in college, at age nineteen. We had our challenges and, in the early stages of our relationship, I was not ready to make a lifelong commitment. However, after being apart for a time, we came back together when we were twenty. Neither of us ever wanted to be with anyone else, and we got married a year after graduation, at age twenty-two. In our circles, that was young.

However, recent research by Brad Wilcox and Lyman Stone suggests that we made the right decision. Wilcox and Stone analyzed the reports of marriage and divorce from more than 50,000 women in the US government's National Survey of Family Growth. Their conclusions show that the least-likely group to experience divorce is women aged twenty to twenty-four who marry without having cohabitated prior to marriage. We were right in the middle of that demographic.

Here are some thoughts on building a long-term relationship. When Melanie and I got married, it was in the context of family, friends, and the church. The weakest kind of promise is one you make to yourself. We have all made New Year's resolutions which we have subsequently broken, often in just days or weeks. The second kind of promise is made to someone else. These tend to last longer, because we feel guilty when we go back on our word, but we still often do and rationalize our reasons for doing so. But when we take a public oath, before God and witnesses, that is often the kind of promise that is upheld.

I talk to couples who are contemplating marriage and suggest they think about a three-strand rope. While one strand is always vulnerable to breaking under pressure, the three strands support each other and can survive a greater tension or load. Likewise, when you understand that, in marriage, you make a promise to yourself, to your spouse, *and* to God and the community, the chances of staying together rise dramatically.

This is not to say that there will never be conflict, hurt feelings, or rough times. But it *is* to say that the unwavering commitment to stay together can overcome any short-term disappointments and drives an overwhelming need for ongoing reconciliation. You must also recognize that over a lifetime, each of you will grow and change. The secret is to do that together, and never let that be an excuse to grow apart.

Melanie and I were young when we got married. Over our entire lives together, we have consistently created space for the other and worked together to achieve things that neither of us could have conceived of on our own. We both had a lot of growing and exploring yet to do. All the while, we were committed to seeking new experiences together.

Research strongly suggests that couples who experience new things together are able to sustain the marriage relationship and experience a wide range of cognitive and romantic benefits. Researchers Arthur and Elaine Aron termed this a sense of self-expansion.

In reviewing this and subsequent research for his book *The Laws of Connection: The Scientific Secrets of Building a Strong Social Network*, David Robson concludes that,

"Self-expansion isn't simply a luxury of youthful court-ship, but an essential feature of any satisfying long-term relationship." Robson goes on to cite other research that shows couples who live in this reality are less inclined to commit infidelity and more likely to experience enhanced romantic connection. He says, "Simply sharing new experiences and activities increased physical desire in long-term partnerships."

Melanie and Frank, Zion National Park

Sharing achievements

The first test of our partnership was my return to business school. Despite being pregnant with our first child,
Melanie took on the role of primary breadwinner. We
moved to a new city, and she continued her career in
marketing. But it was still a partnership. I took on any
job I could to support our budget. During the day, I sold
shoes in Harvard Square at the Tennis and Squash Shop.
At night, I was a Wells Fargo security guard for the soccer
tournament of the 1984 Olympics. Our unarmed security
force must have looked formidable in our paratrooper
khakis from Levi's and our bright blue berets.

Once our daughter was born, I shifted my schedule.
I would drop her off at daycare and pick her up after
classes and studying. I would prepare dinner, and we
would spend a little time together as a family before putting the baby down. I would then return to my studies.

I began meeting my study group early in the morning,
with Melanie dropping off our daughter before work. We
talked openly about money, or lack thereof, and knew we
were accumulating debt. We left Harvard with a negative
net worth of $29,000.

After business school, we were both working but money
was tight. We borrowed money from my sister and bought
a house with three percent down using Federal Housing
Administration (FHA) financing. Maxing out 401(k) contributions, paying down school loans, and making mortgage payments was tough. The end of the month was often
peanut-butter-and-jelly time. Our second child came
along, and Melanie landed a plum flex-time job back with
NCNB. We had a little more breathing room, bought a

new house, and paid off the rest of the loan. After seven years of watching every penny, we were okay.

And then things got crazy. I left my real estate career to lead the Children's Services Network, and Melanie got promoted. In my negotiation with the agency, they matched my current salary and John Crosland hired me as his strategy consultant. With Melanie's promotion, our take-home pay actually went up. Two months later, Melanie was selected for one of three bank scholarships for business school at Queens University.

Now, my holding space for her began. Her classes required that she attend study group every Thursday evening and be in class all day on alternating Fridays and Saturdays. Thursday was my basketball night. Instead of canceling, we adapted. I took the kids to my game, along with some crafts for them, and bought a pizza. The kids loved it. Soon, other dads began bringing their children, and Thursday became a dads-and-kids night at the local gym.

Two months after graduating from her business school, Melanie had the chance to serve as an on-the-ground advisor to Banca Transilvania (BT), a banking institution headquartered in Cluj, Romania. The Iron Curtain had recently fallen, and BT wanted to shift from communist principles to those of Western capitalism. In the middle of Melanie's ten-week sojourn the kids and I visited for two weeks, as we wanted to learn about a new part of the world as a family. Today, that once-fledgling institution has become the largest bank in Romania, with over $35 billion in assets.

My work in the non-profit world had run its course, and I went back into real estate. Melanie was promoted again, to senior vice president. We bought our third house. We began construction on a vacation home. We were both making the most money we'd ever had, but, as things progressed, we were both traveling out of town regularly. Despite more help from Melanie's parents, the path we were on was unsustainable.

Also, Melanie recognized that she needed to create some space for me. My company was taking off, and I had just vested in ownership. After some soul-searching, she decided to resign from the bank and care for our teenagers. That decision allowed me to go full-bore. The company would flourish, go public, and become the nation's largest healthcare design/build firm.

As one child headed to college and the other was in high school, Melanie rekindled her long-dormant interest in all things science. At age forty-six, she began the classes that would lead to her earning a PhD in the new field of bioinformatics. Her path in science culminated in her creation of the Center for Outcomes Research and Evaluation (CORE) for Atrium Health, where she managed thirty-eight researchers working across the nation's second-largest publicly owned health system. Her papers have been cited by other scientists over 1,550 times.

As Melanie headed to graduation in May of 2011, I felt the need to change direction as well.

Me: "Can we talk? There's something I need to tell you."

Melanie: "Sure. What is it?"

Me: "I want to enroll in seminary, and now feels like the right time."

Melanie: "Well, it's about time. I've never met anyone who cares as much about theology as you do."

And so, a week after Melanie received her doctoral hood, I began intensive Hebrew on a journey that would entail almost four years in seminary. For the next several years, I sacrificed every Saturday in pursuit of my Master of Divinity (MDiv). To become a minister in the Presbyterian Church, you have to learn Hebrew and Greek, complete your MDiv, pass ordination exams, receive a job offer, and be examined by your Presbytery.

Melanie made all that possible for me. I would be in class until 5 p.m. each Saturday, then take the next twenty-four hours as Sabbath, during which we spent all our time together. I feel like I almost went backward through seminary. During my second year, my book *The Benefit of the Doubt: Claiming Faith in an Uncertain World* was published. In my third year, I was offered the job of leading the Board of Pensions of the Presbyterian Church (USA). I was ordained as a minister in February of 2015, and, through a scheduling quirk that pushed graduation into April of that year, finally graduated from seminary.

Ordination to Minister of Word and Sacrament

We have both always believed in constant learning. As president of the Board of Pensions, I was leading substantial research into the nature of sustainable ministry in our denomination. When my seminary announced it was restarting its doctoral program with an emphasis on serving in the world, I signed up for the first cohort. Little did I know COVID was about to hit, which sent all courses online and allowed me to control my class schedules and the production of my doctoral thesis. I was awarded my doctorate in April of 2022, and my work has become the cornerstone of transformation at the Board of Pensions.

Doctoral hooding ceremony

Ensuring you don't skip the romance

Throughout our lives together, Melanie and I have maintained an active and fun-filled intimate relationship. This is critical for any marriage to survive. Yes, sex is wonderful, but more importantly, the closeness of physical intimacy keeps you bonded to each other. When desire has waned at times, that very closeness allows you to talk things out. Sharing honestly with each other about desires and anxieties has allowed us to navigate the down times, and stay connected and excited about being together.

Part of maintaining your intimate relationship is creativity and trying new things. Whatever you and your partner enjoy, have fun with it. Like many couples, we have planned getaways that have proven to be wonderful times to reconnect.

But it's not strictly about physical intimacy. Keep the romance alive in other parts of your life, too. Melanie carried Sonia roses in her wedding bouquet. Since then, on every anniversary, I have given her one Sonia rose for each of the years we've been married.

On our thirtieth anniversary, I switched to one white rose for each decade, and Sonia roses for the subsequent years. I've never missed a year, even when we've been away from home. The flowers for our eighteenth anniversary were delivered at the Peninsula Hotel in Hong Kong. The flowers for our thirty-fourth anniversary arrived at the Ocean Club on Paradise Island (our honeymoon hotel), while those for our thirty-ninth anniversary came to the William Gray in Montreal.

Melanie and Frank, 2004

Little surprises count too. I write poetry for Melanie, often delivering my new verses on her birthday by
adding to a special book I gave her years ago. In times
when we have not been together, I have written romantic

material for her eyes only. Once, when we were apart on Valentine's Day, we planned a trip to Paris on phones and laptops, and booked the flights right then. Ahh, Paris.

But the big gestures can create an unforgettable memory. When I had asked Melanie to marry me, I had designed a ring with a high-quality, albeit small, diamond. I wanted to get her a spectacular ring for our twenty-fifth anniversary. While I probably would have done just fine picking out something on my own, I thought it would be more fun to do it together. But how do you make that a surprise?

On the night of the twenty-fifth anniversary of our engagement, a date Melanie had completely forgotten, I booked a private room at one of our favorite restaurants. I arranged for her parents to babysit, and they were waiting for Melanie when she got home from work. They told her to get ready for an evening out, and that a limo would pick her up in an hour.

When she arrived at the restaurant, looking fabulous in a flowing gown, she was escorted to the room where I waited in my tuxedo. We had a marvelous dinner, and, because the twenty-fifth is the silver anniversary, I gave her a silver ring as a promise for the real present. She loves the ring we designed together, but I daresay the memory of how she got it is equally dear.

Our twenty-fifth wedding anniversary celebration six months later involved the four couples with whom we have been close friends for most of our adult lives. All four men had played in that Thursday-night basketball game. We really splurged by renting a villa outside of Siena in the Tuscan hills, and all four couples, plus our young adult children, spent a magical two weeks together.

Four couples, all friends

Doing life together

We have raised two wonderful children who both have families of their own. From the beginning, we have always taken the children with us. It began with our infant daughter in the Snugli at graduate-school events, and that has never stopped. When we taught Wednesday-night church school for disadvantaged children in Charlotte's housing projects, the children went with us and were just part of the class.

We never talked down to the children, but always included them in the conversation, just as my parents had done with me. Melanie's parents were an integral part of our lives, which gave our children multiple adults with whom to bond.

We made a point of exposing the kids to travel and international affairs. We twice hosted former Soviet guests, including Andrey Makarevich, founder of the band Time Machine, who gave us a bootleg album that Paul McCartney recorded live in Moscow. Other guests were Georgian artist Gogi Chagelishvili, who drew pictures of our young son, and a physician who was part of the inner circle serving top government officials. It was that doctor who told us that the leader of the Soviet Union, Yuri Andropov, had been murdered by an irate spouse while he was cracking down on corruption. She shot him in the back, fatally injuring him. The official cause of death was kidney failure.

After the trip to Romania, we added Paris, a study trip to Asia with the McColl School of Business, a grand tour of Europe to celebrate graduations, and the aforementioned two weeks in Italy. As adults, but before we became grandparents, we also did a two-week tour of Croatia with the children and their spouses.

Our children continue to travel the world without us. Our daughter went to Beijing for intensive language study, and her current role as a consultant has taken her to every continent except Antarctica. Our son has traveled extensively in Europe, and his certification in business German saw him land his first job after law school as an associate with a Wall Street law firm. We now have six grandchildren to dote on, and remain very close to both families.

We have had so much fun and adventure together. We have traveled the globe with our family and as a couple. Always together, we have been tennis partners, precinct captains, youth advisors, Odyssey of the Mind coaches,

Family trip to Croatia

team parents, and church school teachers. We have been each other's best friend and most trusted advisor. And we have been lovers for more than forty years.

Our marriage hasn't been perfect, but it has been consistent. It has been a committed partnership from the beginning. At different times, each of us has been the primary breadwinner. At other times, each of us has played the more supportive role. We've made every major decision together. Melanie is more introverted, and I am often an out-front leader, but this partnership is the most important relationship in our lives, and we nurture it and each other.

Frank and Melanie

CHAPTER 7

FINDING AN INTEGRATED LIFE

I will acknowledge that fully integrating all aspects of one's life is not something that is easy, or even practical, at many stages of that life. While the four key elements of my life—family, career, faith, and community—have always been present, at various times some of them have received greater emphasis than others. When I was leading a public company, the time I had for church and community dwindled as I put needed focus on business and family.

Having achieved financial independence and with both children out of college, I was able to realign the amount of time devoted to various facets of my life. Athletic pursuits, intellectual priorities, affordable housing, and service to the Church were all repositioned within the hierarchy of my time.

Drifting

As I was preparing to leave Cogdell Spencer, and with no other employment on the horizon, I gave myself licence to pursue interests long left unattended. Playing golf twice a week enabled me to get down to a nine handicap. I called authors whose books I enjoyed and offered to take them to lunch if they would discuss their work. Most authors love to talk about their books.

I reconnected with everyone who had ever been my pastor, and invited all six to join me for a two-day seminar based on the senior member's sermon on faith and doubt, which he had preached when I was fifteen years old. That sermon gave me permission to bring all questions to God—nothing was off limits, even the seemingly sacrilegious ideas. Amazingly, his associate pastor at the time had saved a copy of that very sermon.

We brought a moderator to the gathering, and everyone agreed that I could record our discussions. I ended up with twenty-four hours of recordings from six Presbyterian ministers, which became the basis of my book *The Benefit of the Doubt* and gave me the assurance that seminary was a viable option.

Toward the end of my first year in seminary, I accepted the job of president of Habitat Charlotte. The affiliate organization was entering its thirtieth year of existence, and it had become such a fixture in Charlotte that a lot of its good work was taken for granted. Volunteers and contributions were on the decline; benefits for the staff had been cut, and salaries were frozen. We decided to reintroduce Habitat to the community, and launched the "30/30/30" initiative: serving thirty families in thirty days with thirty community partners. We negotiated for billboards around town, and banner signs at each of the seven churches that had founded Habitat in Charlotte.

Frank, Habitat International CEO Jonathan Reckford, and Bert Green

The concept caught fire. From church groups to law firms, everyone wanted to participate. Lowe's Companies decided to build a complete home in thirty hours, a process that was covered by local TV. Bank of America gave us a $3 million unsecured line of credit. We ended up serving forty-three families, with 112 community partners, deploying $3 million in funds in the thirty days of the campaign. Habitat Charlotte permanently increased production by fifty percent, and was named one of seven Affiliates of Distinction. I was called to Congress in January of 2014 to testify about mortgage policy for affordable housing.

Habitat Charlotte named an Affiliate of Distinction

Sometimes, it pays to make a fool of yourself. While president of Habitat Charlotte, I was part of a trip to visit our partner affiliate Habitat El Salvador. That particular trip was an annual event that attracted well-heeled supporters. Following a day of work on the house we were building, our hosts had arranged for a private dinner at a local restaurant. As we entered, one of our volunteers noticed the karaoke machine.

He said he would pledge one house in El Salvador ($8,000) if I would sing "Super Freak" by Rick James. I agreed that I would do so after dinner. As dinner progressed, others heard this challenge and wanted in. Two women each pledged a house if they could set the tune. Two others pledged houses if the entire Charlotte staff would be my backup singers. "Call Me Maybe" by Carly Rae Jepsen was selected. With $40,000 raised, we performed with great energy, if not great vocal stylings. Thank goodness no video of the event exists.

While leading Habitat for Humanity in Charlotte and studying to complete my MDiv, I began my term on the investment and audit committees of the Board of Pensions of the Presbyterian Church (USA).

The Board of Pensions is a bit of a misnomer: while it does indeed manage a defined benefit pension plan, it is really a full-service benefits provider. The board was running a nationwide health plan, offering financial protection for death and disability, providing financial education to our members, hosting mid-career discernment conferences for our pastors, and administering the financial assistance fund for church employees and pensioners. The board had about $8 billion in assets when I joined the investment and audit committees.

The perfect combination

When the CEO of the Board of Pensions announced his impending retirement, the chair encouraged me to be a candidate to succeed the CEO. After all, I was bizarrely qualified: multiple CEO positions, an expert in finance and investing, a student of the healthcare system (having served it for fifteen years), a teacher of adults in both the church and the academy, and about to become a Presbyterian minister.

Besides, the chair apparently liked the way I led organizations. He had been a top hospital administrator and a major client of Cogdell Spencer. When he retired from that position, I hired him as our lead consultant in the northeast. So, he had been my customer, my employee, and, if the cards fell in my favor, he would soon be my boss.

While it seemed like a perfect fit in many ways, the job would require moving to Philadelphia. Melanie and I were deeply rooted in the Charlotte community, and her job was still there. After long discussions and some praying, Melanie said to me, "You need to do this for the church." I was offered the job in 2014 and began in June, after being unanimously elected by the biennial general assembly.

My role as a minister and as president of the Board of Pensions has taken me to some wonderful places. Melanie and I represented the Presbyterian Church (USA) at the 150th anniversary of the Presbyterian Church in Taiwan. I was invited to lead worship at St. Giles Cathedral in Edinburgh, Scotland. Presbyterians view St. Giles as the mother church of our denomination, and it was an incredible thrill to robe up in John Knox's vestry.

In the summer of 2023, I was invited to be one of ten preachers for the Summer Worship Series in Montreat, North Carolina. As a lifelong Montreater, I preached a sermon on the legacy of the town, highlighting the wonderful and the shameful aspects of our history and posing the question of what legacy we are leaving to our children and grandchildren.

As a minister, I've married my son and daughter-in-law, presided at the funerals of our parents, preached at our seminaries, celebrated communion, and baptized grandchildren. Ordained ministry has opened a deeply meaningful chapter for me within the church.

Professionally, the Board of Pensions was the perfect fit. Large, complex financial matters to tackle. A steady stream of church-related meetings and invitations to preach. A mission-oriented non-profit serving over 65,000

Celebrating communion

beneficiaries, all of whom had worked in a congregation or other ministry of the church.

I set out to transform the board from an antiquated system offering a single package of benefits into a modern benefits platform. The process touched every aspect of the operations: information technology, creation of sales and marketing, implementation of multiple products, flexibility for employers, and transparency of pricing. We stopped thirty years of declining active membership, and began winning new members.

American Presbyterians are known for having started colleges and universities. We founded seminaries and hospitals. We have created and run conference centers and retirement communities. But many Presbyterians have forgotten this heritage. The Board of Pensions was knitting the church back together.

We also transformed our portfolio management and financial systems. Communications went from all paper and faxes to 100 percent online. We demolished our 7,000-square-foot mail room and built a town center, where staff now gather and often share meals or worship together. Assets topped $13 billion. It took a full ten years and tens of millions of dollars to reshape the organization.

When I began my work at the Board of Pensions I was fifty-four years old, and I told the board of directors that I expected to be there at least twelve years. I had three four-year plans from the beginning: transform healthcare offerings and services for lay employees; transform systems and pursue growth; and complete systems change and succession planning. I knew the entire executive team would turn over during my tenure. I didn't count on having to manage through two years of COVID, change how we care for our ministers, or complete an overhaul of our retiree health plan. Those latter three initiatives simply became a part of fulfilling the mission.

Thinking long term requires commitment to a mission and a vision. Multiple times while president of the board, I have been approached to lead other institutions.

I turned away every opportunity, because my work plan was not complete. Just as I stayed at Children's Services Network because my three goals had not been achieved, so too have I stayed with the Board of Pensions to complete what I have begun.

Hopping from job to job does not ultimately build a career. Achievement of important milestones does. That said, the longest I have been in any one organization is fifteen years, long enough to fulfill goals and often with the aim of transforming the way the organization works. I have been a change agent and pursued my career in discernable chapters, always keeping to a through-line of what is truly important in our lives.

Personal costs

Leading the board wasn't ideal on a personal level. For the first year, I rented an apartment and flew home to Charlotte every weekend. Assuming Melanie would soon be joining me, we bought a house in center-city Philadelphia and sold our house in Charlotte. Melanie is an only child, and her parents became acutely in need of care. We rented her an apartment, and she continued to work at the health system. Her mother passed away a year later.

Instead of this freeing Melanie to join me, her father became even more dependent on her. We kept the apartment a mile from his retirement community. I flew to Charlotte three out of every four weekends. I would visit my mother on Saturdays, and Melanie's father on Sundays.

My mother died in August of 2019, and Melanie scheduled retirement for that fall. We planned a nine-week sabbatical trip to New Zealand and Australia for the spring of 2020. We boarded the plane in Philadelphia on March 11, changed planes at LAX, took off across the Pacific, and passed over the international date line.

By the time we arrived in Auckland on March 13, COVID had been declared a national emergency in the United States. March Madness and the NBA season had been canceled. On March 14, the sixth confirmed case in New Zealand was reported. We didn't know it at the time, but Melanie already had COVID and would have been case number seven had her case been reported. Over the weekend, the City of Philadelphia asked all offices to remain closed.

I told Melanie we would be in Auckland for two more days or two more months—a gross underestimation. Our daughter, pregnant with her second child and desperate to get out of New York City, asked if she could bring her family to our house in Philadelphia.

We caught the last flight from Auckland to LAX at almost midnight on March 18. One week later, New Zealand went into total lockdown. It took us thirty hours and a detour through San Francisco to get home. We holed up with our daughter's family for four months, as Melanie's father was likewise quarantined in his retirement community.

The Board of Pensions initiated its business continuity plan, with everyone working from home on laptops. Our executive team gathered every day at 3 p.m. on Microsoft Teams to review where we were and solve problems to keep us up and running. At home, three of us were working remotely while Melanie, still suffering from long COVID, saw to the needs of our two-year-old grandson.

When her father's continuing-care facility designated her as his caregiver the following fall, Melanie returned to Charlotte and our dual-city relationship resumed. Years earlier, we had promised each other that we would give whatever it took to keep our relationship at the forefront. That we did, but things like golf and building friendships in new cities fell by the wayside, and Melanie's life was similarly constrained. Her father passed away in early 2021. We have been together ever since.

When my work at the Board of Pensions is complete, we will eventually move back to Charlotte and be home again. Melanie is still a member of our home church there, and I am still an active member of the Charlotte Presbytery. We fully expect that we will re-engage in the community and spend the last third of our lives working to build it into a better place, just as our long-time friends and mentors have done before us.

CHAPTER 8

LOOKING AHEAD

Most of what I have described in this book has come from my direct experience, and is therefore inherently backward-looking. However, my role in leading organizations has been to synthesize information, look forward, and create a vision for the future. As hockey legend Wayne Gretzky famously said when asked about his uncanny ability to score goals, "I skate to where the puck is going, not where it is." Predicting the future is always risky, but in your life and career it's essential nonetheless. Those who prefer to take things as they come are inevitably followers, and do not help to create the reality in which they wish to live.

Generational shifts

In my current organization, I lead a team that has four generations represented: Baby Boomers, Generation X, Millennials, and Generation Z. Each group has positive characteristics, which often come with their own sets of idiosyncrasies.

Dr. Bea Bourne of Purdue University Global is a recognized expert on generational differences. She characterizes the world view of generations as follows:

- **Boomers**: believe that achievement comes after paying one's dues; sacrifice for success.

- **Xers**: favor diversity; quick to move on if their employer doesn't meet their needs; resistant to change at work if it affects their personal lives.

- **Millennials**: seek challenges, growth, and development; prioritize a fun work-life balance; likely to leave an organization if they don't like changes.

- **Gen Z**: self-identify as digital device addicts; value independence and individuality; prefer to work with Millennial managers, innovative co-workers, and new technologies.

I have developed my own opinions through managing colleagues in all four groups.

My generation, the Boomers, are often characterized as those dedicated to work and achievement. The rise of the "company man" is emblematic of our generation. We are also critiqued for an overemphasis on material goods and financial security. Younger generations see us as loyal to institutions and the keepers of the status quo. But our generation was the generation of tremendous social change. We were the generation that believed in free love, protested the Vietnam War, championed women's liberation, and pushed the civil rights agenda that

reshaped the United States. All of those things are true
at once.

The Gen Xers have often been portrayed as being left
behind in the Boomers' wake. Now in their forties and
fifties, many have not seen the same kind of financial
and organizational successes that the Boomers enjoyed.
Often, they still find themselves reporting to Boomers,
whom they see as standing in the way. I hear this in business circles but also in the church, where Gen Xers see
Boomers remaining in the pulpits that the younger group
deeply desires to fill. The Gen Xers never really abandoned faith in the institutions they now want to lead, but
are disappointed by a lack of opportunity.

The Millennials are quite a different story. Most grew
up with Boomer parents, and there is a distinct divide in
how they view the world. Many are iconoclasts, devoted
to tearing down the very institutions their parents built.
In fact, I would say this describes the majority of this generation. They are the employees who most often want to
work remotely, have accepted the idea of a gig economy,
and no longer believe in the effectiveness of government,
church, or cultural institutions. They attempt to separate
work and life, devoting as little as is required to the former and building social circles to create the latter. They
are not lazy by any stretch, but deeply disillusioned by
the state of things and therefore determined to forge a
path independent of the perceived Boomer values. At its
extreme, this attitude finds voice in those calling for the
end of capitalism as an economic system.

However, at the other extreme within the Millennials is a minority that, instead of rejecting the Boomer
values, has embraced them. They were high achievers

in school, reinforced by their parents' praise. They have come roaring out of colleges and graduate schools into those institutions and businesses that so many of their contemporaries have given up on. As leaders have recognized their work ethic, drive, inherent productivity, and comfort with technology, they are being promoted and rewarded at increasing rates. Many are now managing teams of Gen Xers, and they are starting to hire and guide the Gen Z members who are following them. Like it or not, when it comes to careers, they will leave many of their own generation behind.

That brings us to Gen Z, the digital natives. This generation has never known a world without the internet, social media, and instant access to information. Why memorize information that is easily accessible on your smartphone? Some in this group will undoubtedly find fulfillment and financial success in the digital world through apps or influencing. But that is not where the real action will be. This coming era will be the age of artificial intelligence.

Artificial intelligence

Gen Z is the generation that will shape how our world uses artificial intelligence (AI). In turn, AI will be shaped not by individuals and influencers, but by the large organizations that have access to capital and can afford to invest. This trend is already apparent in the capital markets. Meta, Amazon, Microsoft, Alphabet, Salesforce, and Apple are already dominating the research and implementation of AI.

AI will fundamentally change the way we think about business, and almost every other element of our cultural landscape. What might lie ahead?

The first issue that we must confront in the whole generative AI discussion is the concept of the learning set. I have heard this debated at multiple forums and panels, and I have come to appreciate this as fundamental. The positions around this generally fall along a spectrum: from a highly restrictive learning set to, in contrast, a vast learning set that includes the internet and all private data, which gets loaded into a large language model (LLM) like ChatGPT, developed by OpenAI.

Those who argue for highly restrictive learning sets see AI primarily as a productivity tool, the uses of which should be highly controlled. A good example of this is the use of chatbots in customer service online interfaces. If your questions are germane to the service you are engaging with (think cable TV or insurance), then the answers are already highly reliable. Ask a question that is outside those set parameters, and you get no answer at all.

At the other end of the spectrum, enthusiasts want to create an all-knowing, human-like persona. Author and speaker Calum Chace predicts that this kind of AI will create two singularities: a jobless economy, and a super-intelligence that will drive both virtual reality and real-world human behavior. He hopes that the super-intelligence will have consciousness, so that it will have compassion and not destroy us.

While this kind of godlike omnipotence can be tempting, and fascinating, the outcomes are highly variable. I have experimented with these large language models, and sometimes they seem almost magical; at other times, their answers are either wrong or nonsensical. What most people find is that the more defined the question is, the better the answer.

The first question I ever asked ChatGPT was a theological one. I wrote, "Write an essay explaining Karl Barth's corrective to John Calvin's doctrine of predestination." The answer I got back was astounding, and I sent it to a friend who I knew loved this topic. She wrote back, "Best I have ever seen." My conclusion was that very few scholarly articles have been written on this subject, and the ones that have are created by theologians who generally knew what they were talking about. Therefore, ChatGPT's learning set for this very specific and detailed question was limited and contained no disinformation, as many online sources unfortunately do.

As of this writing, ChatGPT often gives very generic answers, particularly when questions are broad and the learning set is vast. On many questions, especially concerning predictions or uncertainty, it declines altogether, although I foresee a time when probabilistic forecasts will become common. After all, these are the substance of everything from weather forecasts (apps already tell us next week's weather) to potential outcomes in sports and elections.

The first place I believe we will see widespread use of these language-based AI tools is in translation between languages. They are already quite adept in most modern languages. Within the next few years, I believe we will see every electronic document immediately available in the user's preferred language. Unlike the word-for-word translations in apps like Google Translate, these new tools will render the document as a native reader or speaker would express the concepts. We will see this first on webpages, and then for any document. Close on the heels of this will be emails and messages composed in the sender's language and received in the language of the recipient. Not far behind will be real-time spoken-language translation, the universal translator of *Star Trek* come to life.

One real constraint that we may face is the speed at which infrastructure can adapt to the new technology of AI. High demands for power to push these systems is already outstripping our ability to produce electricity. The solution of bringing dormant nuclear power generators, such as Three Mile Island, back online is only one example of power companies looking at every possible mechanism to meet demand, which is growing exponentially.

This huge power requirement is due to the structure of current AI technology, which requires the software to review the entire learned set in response to each question. Human brains only turn on the neurons associated with the information that is relevant to the question or stimulus. Data scientists are working on this kind of neural-net processing for AI, which could greatly reduce the energy demand for the lightning-fast answers we all want. These potential breakthrough solutions are unlikely before the strain on infrastructure becomes a limiting factor.

Diversity and the future of work

What does all this portend for the world of work? Broadly stated, anything that is currently created by typing on a keyboard will be replaced by AI, which can do it faster and more accurately. As digital natives, Gen Z will have an initial advantage on the aging Xers, but digital fluency will be assumed going forward and will never again be a distinguishing characteristic. It will be as fundamental to the next generation of leaders as reading and writing skills were to my contemporaries.

Ironically, the more that technology becomes ubiquitous, the more important human interaction will become. Technicians will always be able to find a job, but leaders will arise through other means. Leaders, whether in business, politics, or culture, will be those who can inspire and persuade. There is no substitute for personal interaction.

When I was contemplating joining the Cogdell Group in late 1995, Jim asked me if I could sell, in part because my approach was so different from his own. There are many types of selling, and almost all human endeavors require some element of sales. I don't mean this in the sense of convincing someone to buy something they don't need or want, but rather helping them meet their needs or achieve their goals.

I was fortunate to take a course on selling when I was still early in my career. It was based on what was then known as the "Xerox selling principles." The entire course revolved around needs-satisfaction selling. The idea is to engage a potential client in conversation around their goals and whatever their organizational priorities might be, rather than simply stating all of your company or product benefits while you hope to hit on a hot button.

When someone states a need, whatever it may be, the key to selling is being able to meet that need or solve that problem. In my business serving the medical community, I would often focus on the provider's desires. I would ask how many patients they might see in a day, or how many surgeries they might perform. Physicians have only their time to generate revenue, and thus I would focus on increasing their efficiency rather than how much our buildings might cost to construct. Construction costs are similar per square foot, but our designs often resulted in double-digit gains in efficiency that went straight to the provider's bottom line.

This approach to engagement is effective regardless of the pursuit. The best development officers (fundraisers) focus on helping the potential donor fulfill their charitable desires, not just blurting out the great things the organization does. They are meeting a need. The same is true for engaging employers who want to provide benefits for their employees. They don't care about how we negotiate with our vendors—they want to know what the experience will be for their employees, and then what it will cost. This approach is universal. It works in banking, consulting, professional services, investing, and the nonprofit world.

Needs-satisfaction selling depends on one critical element: personal engagement. No amount of technology can replace the power of person-to-person engagement. People do business with other people, and, perhaps more importantly, with people they like. Your ability to create and sustain personal relationships will be the determining factor in organizational success and personal happiness.

Employees have needs as well. To be an effective leader, to inspire colleagues to work hard and provide their best to the organization, you have to meet their needs. We all have the need of sufficient income; that is a given. But that is not why employees are engaged with their organizations. They need to believe in the vision and mission of an organization. They need to trust the leaders setting the direction. They need to feel that they are cared for as human beings. None of that—a shared vision, trust, care—happens without face-to-face engagement.

Whether selling to potential customers, managing a team, or leading an organization or community movement, the constituencies will be ever more diverse. You only have to look at global changes that are already underway. India has now surpassed China as the most populous nation in the world, while Nigeria is already among the top ten. In the United States, the fastest-growing segment of the population is Hispanic. All of these shifts will be reflected in the workplace and in community groups. This means different races, different religions, different ethnic customs, and very different lived experiences.

I grew up in a geography that defined diversity as African American or white. In fact, the court order that ended racial segregation required the school system to track data in only two categories: "Black" and "Others." My small town was entirely Protestant Christian. To my recollection, there were neither Catholics nor Jews. And yet, the many opportunities to experience desegregation, and talk about those issues, prepared me for an openness that would later prove instrumental in my commitment to diversity, equity, and inclusion.

Madeline Hunter was my sixth-grade teacher. She was also the first African American teacher I had studied under. Mrs. Hunter led us in open discussions of race and prejudice. We watched *Brian's Song*, a movie that detailed the friendship between Gayle Sayers and Brian Piccolo, two running backs of different races who played for the Chicago Bears. Explicitly dealing with the racial tensions in our community was part of the curriculum.

In these matters, my parents had a deep influence. Instead of putting me in one of the "white flight" private schools, my parents fully embraced the public school experience. I watched as my father worked to bring racial diversity to the Davidson College student body and faculty. He was a founding member of the board of directors of the Urban League in Charlotte. I was on hand as an adult when he was presented with their highest honor, the Whitney M. Young Jr. Award.

It was when Melanie and I moved to Cambridge, Massachusetts that I was first made aware of a wide range of prejudice and discrimination that was invisible to me in North Carolina. I was working in Harvard Square at the Tennis and Squash Shop. As I chatted up a woman who wanted new tennis shoes, I commented that it was a wonderful thing that a major party had finally nominated a woman, Geraldine Ferraro, for vice president. She said, "I suppose so, but I could never vote for an Italian." I was stunned, having never encountered anything like ethnic prejudice instead of racial discrimination.

My own experiences in sports, student government, my fraternity, community service, affordable housing, the Chamber of Commerce, and Habitat for Humanity have all shaped me. One profound experience occurred during my seminary days. I did a one-on-one semester with Professor Rodney Sadler, an African American scholar who has written extensively on race and scripture. We unpacked our different experiences and our common intersections. He helped me realize that things such as family heritage, seemingly simple for me, were a hallmark of privilege. He shared that virtually no African Americans can trace heritage before their ancestors arrived in the United States as enslaved people.

When it comes to matters of race and equity among the Millennials and Gen Z, the best analogy I have ever heard was presented by *New York Times* opinion writer Leonard Pitts. At a conference in Montreat, Pitts described a journey of two Boomer friends, one white, one African American. They decide to travel together with a goal of achieving equity: their current reality, represented by Miami, and the place of full realization, represented by Seattle. In other words, two places far apart.

So, these two friends get in the car and they go a long way, arriving in Kansas City. They get out and stay for years. For many reasons, the journey does not continue. While they both agree that where they are is much better than the place they left, it is not where they originally hoped to go. At this point in the story, Pitts says:

> *"Folks, the Millennial generation was born in Kansas City. They've heard about Miami, but never lived there. From their perspective, nothing has ever happened to change their reality, and maybe they've seen Kansas City has gotten worse. This is why they don't value the institutions or cultural progress that the Boomers do."*

These experiences have created a deep passion for diversity, equity, and inclusion in my work life. We have put those beliefs to work at the Board of Pensions, where changes in policy and practice have resulted in significant progress in creating a more diverse and more talented leadership team.

A few critics, and a few well-meaning but misguided progressives, have commented on our work in diversity assuming that, somehow, we make allowances for the people of color we have added to our ranks. I always respond the same way: "The process has increased our talent by creating a much wider pool of top candidates. We always pick the smartest, best-qualified candidates. To do anything less is to diminish all candidates."

And so, the world of work will be ever more driven by technology, but those who lead will not be distinguished by technology. Personal relationships will drive outcomes at both the individual and organizational level. For the next generation of leaders, that will necessarily require an ability to forge commonality and true friendships across lines of race, religion, sexual identity, and ethnicity.

The world is wide open for the members of Gen Z who want to claim it. Technology will make many things easier, and eliminate many roles that are built around processing information. For those who build the people skills, develop the leadership attributes, grow confident with public speaking, and show a willingness to engage with a wide diversity of people in the community as well as with customers and clients, the sky is the limit, and I am eager to see what wonders they create.

I described my experience with mentors who were older than I was. I recommend a mentoring relationship for those early in their careers now. But leave Boomers out of your equation—and, likewise, avoid the disenchanted Gen Xers. Find a Millennial leader who is already moving into the top echelon of their organization. They are out there: I see them all the time in real estate, technology, politics, consulting, accounting, and even the church. They are eager to share, and they will be the leaders you first work beside, and eventually replace.

CONCLUSION
REFLECTIONS ON PRINCIPLES

The principles of commitment, compassion, and curiosity manifest themselves throughout organizational realities and the structures by which we coordinate activity to pursue missional goals. Embracing those principles in your own life requires that you understand how organizations function, commit to developing skills that make you irreplaceable, step forward for leadership, and allow your faith to inform all your choices.

Having moved often between the non-profit and the profit-seeking sectors, I have concluded that each holds valuable lessons for the other. The non-profit sector is of course mission-driven, and attracts those who seek deeper meaning in their work. The profit-seeking organization has the benefit of a never-ceasing need for efficiency to increase productivity to continue to drive profit growth. Each also has profound deficits, but both can be improved by utilizing a new way of thinking about the intersection of mission and operations.

Envisioning a new paradigm

In all four non-profit organizations I have led, I discovered that leaders feared conflict far more than they cared about efficiency. These organizations tamp down conflict by maintaining strict operating silos. If department heads each control their own operations and budgets, and everyone respects those boundaries, then everyone can pretend to like each other, even when they don't. What is lost is the ability to evaluate where resources should go to enhance total outcomes.

Each time I led one of these organizations, I have had to break down those silos, insisting on joint decision-making and total organizational resource allocation—in other words, bringing the principle of efficiency to the non-profit world. In instances where the organization is small, the impact is correspondingly small. When I arrived at Habitat Charlotte, where we were serving eighty families a year at the time, I first focused on the efficiency of the existing organization, pointing out that if we could be four percent more efficient then we could serve three more families, changing those families' lives.

But the big gains at Habitat Charlotte came when processes were redesigned to function as a whole. We uncoupled fundraising from the construction of a specific house. Instead of making the volunteers raise the money, which slowed us down, we found groups who would give money but had no volunteers, and volunteers to build who had limited money.

Likewise, we grouped our houses together to cut down on travel time, allowing a single superintendent to double their number of projects under management. We gave each of them digital tablets that were tied into our ordering systems in order to speed up review. Volume increased fifty percent, to 120 families per year. As highlighted earlier, we were named one of seven national Affiliates of Distinction.

The profit-seeking side often lacks an understanding of its purpose beyond making money. When I joined the Cogdell organization, the entire team thought their jobs were to have buildings constructed and then manage them, collecting rent, cleaning out toilets, repainting, tending to landscaping, and so on.

I changed all of that. At our first company-wide meeting, I developed a presentation to focus on Michael, a three-year-old cancer patient who got all his care in one of our facilities. Michael's cheer was "Chemo get cancer!" We put Michael's pictures up in our lobby along with the slogan, "We cheer for Michael." The team came to understand their mission as creating facilities that enhanced healing and provided doctors with services so that they could focus on providing care. The drive for efficiency began to contribute to something greater than making money.

These conclusions led me to the development of a new organizational paradigm: product, profit, process. With slight tweaks in wording, this paradigm can apply equally to both non-profit and for-profit organizations.

Product—Whatever the organization produces, whether a physical product or a service, it must meet a real and legitimate need. The greater the need and the more fully that need is met, the better the product. There are many examples of products that have disappeared that either never met a deep need (pet rocks) or have been replaced (8-track tapes). The same is true for services that are often the subject of similar disruption (the full-service stockbrokers of bygone years, and branch banks closing today). Habitat for Humanity meets the deep need of affordable housing just as Cogdell Spencer met the need for modern and affordable healing spaces.

Profit—To survive, a business must make a profit. For a non-profit, we might substitute "sustainable revenue" for profit. After all, no margin, no mission. But it is not simply the organization that needs to profit: everyone who interacts with the organization should be better off than before. This applies to suppliers, business partners, customers, investors, and employees. Viewing the world as a zero-sum game is a loser's attitude, because it destroys any chance at loyalty and long-term relationships.

Michael Porter of Harvard Business School says,

> *"Profit is the magic. Why? Because that profit allows whatever solution we've created to be infinitely scalable. Because if we can make a profit, we can do it for 10, 100, a million, 100 million, a billion. The solution becomes self-sustaining. That's what business does when it makes a profit."*

Process—If we believe our product or service meets a real need, and we can deliver that product or service in a way that leaves everyone better off, then we are morally obligated to perfect the process. On the one hand, organizational practice must reinforce the values on which the fulfillment of the need is based. On a personal level, we must commit to our own excellence. We are obligated to become experts at what we do. This requires continuous learning, attention to detail, and an attitude of hospitality toward all with whom we interact.

Here's a quick summary of the three Ps:

- **Product**—meeting a real need or solving a real problem.

- **Profit**—meeting the need at a price that is sustainable and leaves all involved better off.

- **Process**—becoming expert and ever more effective in meeting the need.

These principles drive the success of all organizations.

Organizational realities

"Must be present to win." You may have heard this phrase in a prize-drawing context. It is absolutely true in organizations as well. There is no substitute for showing up and being present. It is the person who steps forward and volunteers who is noticed—not just for their audacity in the moment, but also for their ensuing work and leadership. My father once told me, "Make sure you are always underpaid." Sounds like bad advice, but he meant contribute more than you take from any organization. When you do, rewards will flow your way.

Take responsibility and execute before you seek a promotion or expect a raise. This is the first principle of gaining professional respect. The leaders who are making decisions about your role in any organization watch for this pattern.

Try to place yourself as close to the decision-makers as possible. If there is a headquarters, try to get there. I had a great vice president who I wanted to promote to be one of three regional property management leaders. He asked if he could do that job without moving to the city with the main office. I said yes, but it would limit his chances to move up further. He joined us at headquarters and ultimately came to run all management nationwide.

The same problem exists with remote work. Out of sight, out of mind. If your remote work consists of typing on a keyboard, you have commoditized yourself. There are literally millions of people around the world who can type just as creatively or brilliantly. According to a survey by Resume Now, forty-six percent of respondents regret being a remote worker. While technology has created options for working locations, it should be viewed as a temporary or periodic option and never a substitute for building personal relationships.

You can't shine on a Zoom call the way you can in a face-to-face meeting. You don't get the side interactions that you find at the office. The serendipitous opportunities to volunteer, collaborate, or take leadership will pass you by. Recent studies now conclude that those who work in an exclusively remote environment get promoted at a significantly lower rate than those who work at the office. *The Wall Street Journal* reports that they are also the first to get laid off.

Leaders often have to make tough decisions when not every member of the team is right for their position. I used to provide intensive coaching, trying to fix problems, helping people get better in their role. More often than not, that ended up hurting the individual and the team suffered as well. I have now come to believe that jobs should not be people's identities, and that ending a bad situation helps both sides move on to a better place.

As a manager, as soon as you lose confidence in someone on your team, you should let them go. If you continue to work with them, you will find they fulfill your worst expectations. It is a vicious cycle, because they are experiencing failure and you are getting more frustrated. My biggest mistakes over forty years have been not acting quickly enough as soon as I diagnosed the problem.

That is not to say that organizations should disregard the needs of employees. In many cases, I have approved moving someone to an easier job as both the organization and the individual waited for retirement. In other cases, helping someone qualify for disability can relieve them of the struggle of trying to keep up. With younger colleagues, offering outplacement services should be the norm.

But there is another kind of personnel problem that takes real courage to face. What if someone is doing what the job calls for, and has a positive attitude, but really won't be happy in the long term because the job is not a good fit for them? This is especially hard with smart people, because they will often produce what you are seeking, even if their heart is not in the job.

The key is honesty. You have to ask them what they want long term and be honest about what the prospects in your organization are. The best way to deal with this is to make it clear that if they keep helping you in their current role, you will help them get the role they want, even if it is in another organization. Everyone with whom I have taken this approach has been grateful and remained a friend long after departure.

I have used this mutual honesty to move a marketing director to a bigger company, a broker to start his own business, a non-profit president to rediscover his passion, a CFO to become successful for another company, and an educator to find her calling, to name just a few.

Remaining loyal to people is a long-term key to both happiness and staying connected in positive ways. When Cogdell Spencer was eventually sold to Ventas, most of the key executives were initially retained. However, over time, layoffs occurred up and down the ladder. Although the executives at Ventas knew nothing about my commitment, I made it my business to help everyone who lost their job find another one, if they wanted it. Not a single person remained unemployed.

That work continued for years following the sale of our company. This approach was not exactly the same as what I had watched John Crosland implement, but I felt it was the right thing to do. It was also my reputation on the line, because I had hired most of them in the first place.

Alumni from the organizations I have led have gone on to even greater positions. Some have stayed in the public company world, rising to chief investment officer or chief accounting officer. Others have gone on to be CFOs, COOs, chief marketing officers, and division executives. Seven have become CEOs or senior equity partners in their own private companies. Still others have had leadership careers in the non-profit world.

Treat people with respect, like the adults they are. I have never tried to manage the schedules of the people who report to me. I realize there are certain jobs, in retail or customer-facing positions, that require fixed hours. But for professionals, focus on their production, not their attendance. If a professional needs to go to a doctor's appointment or attend to a personal matter, you shouldn't care as long as they are meeting their deadlines with quality work.

On a much smaller scale, I have removed vending machines in every organization I have led. Maybe I am remembering the nickel sodas at the weekly paper, but we put in refrigerators and keep them stocked with drinks. The first week or two it is a mad rush to get free drinks, but then it settles down to normal consumption levels. We also buy food whenever a meeting goes into lunch. Little things can make a big difference.

Keeping the saw sharp

Once you develop personal expertise, your options expand greatly. It is essential that you develop marketable skills ahead of opting for long-term career choices that will limit you. When I was president of Habitat, numerous young people came to me saying,

"I want to get into non-profit management."

"That's not a thing," I would answer. "Habitat didn't want me because I have a big heart for people who need houses. They wanted me because I knew finance, construction, fundraising, marketing, and people management. They needed a leader with the skills I had developed."

Graduate schools that are marketing their non-profit management programs are doing their students a disservice. Management and leadership are the same, wherever they are applied. As former White House chief of staff Erskine Bowles told our daughter, "Once you get hard skills, you can always go soft, but it is virtually impossible to go the other way." In that same survey of career regrets by Resume Now, forty-nine percent of all workers regret not ever getting a graduate degree.

I recently had a conversation with a colleague who left for-profit venture capital to lead business creation for a university. He shared that after more than a decade in academia, he couldn't even get an interview on the for-profit side. I have been able to move seamlessly from one sphere to the other because I have always kept a foot in both camps.

While I led Children's Services Network, I continued consulting in real estate strategy and finance. While I was at Cogdell Spencer, I was chair and interim president of Montreat Conference Center. While president of Habitat Charlotte, I was running my own investment company. Now, as I'm at the Board of Pensions, the investment company is still operating, albeit with less active work and more passive structures.

In his book *The 7 Habits of Highly Effective People*, Stephen Covey urges us to "sharpen the saw." By this he means continue to work on yourself through ongoing learning. At every stage of your career, keep reading, and keep going to professional development conferences and classes. I have mentioned a lot of my own professional development throughout these pages: community college, management seminars, continuing education in real estate, master's and doctoral degree programs. I have also pursued other forms that are not so obvious.

For example, I accompanied the Crosland CFO to a week-long class on portfolio theory taught by Roger Ibbotson, Yale School of Management professor and founder of Ibbotson Associates. I used that data to write two articles, both on the expected return on real estate, which were published in national periodicals. I spent a week at the Bell Institute for Leadership while serving as president of Cogdell Spencer. When I came to the Board of Pensions, I took a certificate course in population health at Thomas Jefferson University to become more familiar with running a health plan.

No matter the subject matter, seminars and courses have always broadened my perspective and given me new insight into my own organization or career. Recently, Melanie and I attended two invitation-only Renaissance Weekend gatherings, which bring together a diverse collection of experts in their fields. Everyone presents, and everyone is a learner. It is four days of expanding the mind. We keep investing in ourselves.

I was fortunate to study under the renowned strategist Michael Porter at Harvard Business School. If I could recommend one of his books, it would be the first, *Competitive Strategy*. In it, Porter puts forth his groundbreaking conception of the five forces which determine profitability in all industries: supplier power, buyer power, potential entrants, substitute products and services, and internal competition. The principles in that book have shaped and guided much of my career.

In addition to business books, I read novels and biographies, as well as books on theology, history, and sociology. I stay informed on national, political, and international affairs. All of this broadens my thinking as a leader.

Travel if you can. Whether it is to a state you have never visited or to a foreign country, travel will provide experiences that will illuminate your mind. As part of my participation in the Urban Land Institute, I have visited the forty largest cities in the United States. I have been to two different countries with Habitat for Humanity, and twenty others traveling with family.

As our income rose, so did our standards and means of travel. But I started traveling long before I had any substantial disposable income. I studied abroad, living in a dorm and relying on rail passes and hitchhiking to get around. When Melanie and I were twenty-eight, we took advantage of our last year of Eurail pass eligibility, spending seventeen days seeing the great sights of Europe. To save money on lodging, we planned our route so that we could spend half of our nights on the train.

Talk to other people, network. Networking is a way of being present, but it is also how you are visible in a community. You will discover common interests. I have found many business connections that have developed into long-term relationships. When I first arrived in Philadelphia, I joined one of the local business clubs and soon volunteered to serve on the board. I have met business partners for the Board of Pensions there, and even future employees.

The role of the leader

They say you can exercise leadership at any level of an organization, and in one sense that is true. But being the primary leader of an organization is something quite different. For over thirty years, I have been the executive director, partner, president, or CEO for eight different organizations. Each role has taught me new things, but there are also distinct commonalities.

The first task of leadership is to cast a vision. This is true whether the organization is profit-seeking, non-profit, or religious. Casting a vision is not a majority-rules project, nor should it be relegated to strategic planning retreats among the executive few. It is the leader's job to cast a vision, repeatedly. You know it resonates if others follow you. If the vision doesn't inspire, it is probably the wrong choice.

The second responsibility of the leader is to acquire the resources needed to implement the vision. Resources include the right combination of talent, capital, communications, and customers. This is complex in any organization, and will determine the success or failure of the leader. Particularly in the non-profit world, I have always contended that the right idea will find funding.

The third element of leadership that completes the required trinity is tone at the top. Auditors use this phrase to describe ethical behavior. Organizational development professionals look for consistency of the leader's actions with the stated values of the organization.

If the leader is ethical and will not tolerate anything else, the organization will respond in kind. The same goes for culture and management style. If expectations are that every employee must be devoted to the enterprise above all else, then the culture will reflect unbalanced work-life relationships. Conversely, when the leader demonstrates a commitment to human wholeness, the organization will as well.

A leader's trust is a very fragile thing. The clearest example I can offer is former secretary of state General Colin Powell and the consequences of his losing trust in those to whom he reported and those who reported to him. Allow me to elaborate.

I pulled into a service station on February 5, 2003. It was early afternoon and I was on the way back from a meeting, but I wanted to listen carefully to General Powell's presentation to the United Nations Security Council. He detailed the intelligence that showed unequivocally that Iraq had developed weapons of mass destruction. The US military invasion of that country was therefore a necessary and unavoidable step in the War on Terror. If the United States hesitated, the entirety of Western civilization was at risk. He was compelling, and thus convinced the Security Council, and me. It was the first time I recall hearing about the "coalition of the willing," a phrase that has now become ubiquitous in the business world.

Two years later, General Powell was the guest of honor and keynote speaker at a dinner that Cogdell Spencer was hosting for our client, Roper Hospital, and its doctors. As we listened to the disillusioned general over dinner, it was clear that he was both angry and wounded. He talked about that presentation to the Security Council. He now knew he had been given falsified intelligence, but had trusted the president and his own colleagues. A resolute soldier his whole career, his loyalty had been destroyed in that one incident. Beneath his ever-present military decorum, it was easy to see he was seething.

Melanie and Frank with Colin Powell

The leader cannot check every detail, and so must rely on information provided by others. It is critical that, as a team member, you never shade the truth, manipulate the data, or allow your leader to proceed on a false assumption. As the leader, you have an obligation to check out the facts before proceeding. General Powell wished he had done his own due diligence. My team often jokes that I am the quality assurance department. I review our website. I follow our social media. I never allow my name to have a VIP tag among our vendors, because I want to experience the same customer service as our members.

Despite the jokes, no one wants to get a note from me about things that are wrong, broken, or worse. They all hope they can fix problems before I find them. But I never call people out in public. It is always private, always one on one. I say, "I know you want this right more than I do." And it always gets attention without breaking trust or causing public embarrassment.

A final word

I realized that I could put my faith to work by creating a culture that values the whole lives of people. I tell every employee who comes to work with the Board of Pensions the following things:

- You are here because we expect you to be excellent at your job. No one has ever run into my office and said, "Frank, I want to hire the most mediocre candidate I can find."

- I have noticed that people who are always on dead-line, can barely keep their nose above water, and don't return emails and phone calls in a timely manner, are really not excellent at what they do. If you are excellent, you have some amount of slack in your schedule.

- That slack is important because that is when we reflect on how things could be done better. It's when we learn, both formally and informally, from each other. And most importantly, it's when we extend hospitality—to our customers, to our business partners, and to each other as colleagues.

- I define hospitality in the tradition of the ancient Near East. When the traveler comes, do they need cool water? Do they need to wash off the dirt from the road? Do they need food? And, perhaps most importantly, do they need a safe place to rest? Hospitality means finding out the other person's needs, and then meeting those needs.

- Everyone's life is bigger than this organization. Sometime during your work here, you will be pulled away— to care for a child or parent, to address a personal situation, to be at a joyous event like a birth or wedding. We will provide space for your absence by rallying around to get the work done. If we are all running at 100 percent, we can't extend hospitality by picking up slack.

- When we work with excellence and extend hospitality, people experience grace. That is how they know we represent the church.

Then I tell them this story:

Sometimes I get a phone message that the caller only wants to talk with the president. Those are generally not going to be pleasant conversations. But my direct line is on every email and letter, and I return every call.

Several months earlier, we had decided to send all 20,000 pensioners a gold lapel pin and a letter from me, thanking them for their ministry. Many don't get a formal retirement celebration. It took about eight weeks to create the initial list, order the pins, print the letters, stuff the envelopes, and have them delivered.

During those eight weeks, the caller's husband had died. She began, "How dare you send my dead husband a pin. I won't ever wear it. I think I should just send it back."

"I'm so sorry for your loss," I said, thinking this is a lot of anger over a pin.

But she wasn't mad about the pin. It turned out that no one from the Presbytery had visited her husband in his final weeks. She was mad at the church.

I asked her about where they had served in ministry. I learned about her two sons, who now had families of their own. We laughed about some of the funny things that befall the preacher's wife. We talked for about forty-five minutes, and I could tell we were reaching the end.

"May I ask you a question?" I queried.

"Of course," she answered.

"Why did you want to talk to me?"

"Well," and she paused for a moment, "yours is the only letter I have ever gotten from the national church, and your name and number were right there. So, I thought I would call."

I said, "Well, I'm glad you did."

"I'm glad I did too," she responded, and we said goodbye.

I have no idea what else I worked on that day, but I have never forgotten that caller. In that moment, I was the only person who could give her the care she needed. These same principles of excellence and hospitality apply in building undying customer loyalty in a for-profit business. It is why the last three organizations I have led all won "Best Places to Work" designations. This all circles back around to the three key traits that are required for success in business and happiness in life.

Have you made a **commitment** to excellence in whatever you undertake?

Do you express **compassion** by extending hospitality to all?

Does your **curiosity** drive you to be a constant learner, ever broadening your skills and perspectives?

When the answers to all three questions are, "Yes, all the time," you will find satisfaction in everything you do. You will build the great career and live the happy life you have always wanted.